Cardinal Hayes States Purpose of Catholic Hour

EXTRACT FROM HIS ADDRESS AT THE INAUGURAL PROGRAM

IN THE STUDIO OF THE NATIONAL BROADCASTING COMPANY

NEW YORK CITY, MARCH 2, 1930

Our congratulations and our gratitude are extended to the National Council of Catholic Men and its officials, and to all who, by their financial support, have made it possible to use this offer of the National Broadcasting Company. The heavy expense of managing and financing a weekly program, its musical numbers, its speakers, the subsequent answering of inquiries, must be met.

This radio hour is for all the people of the United States. To our fellow-citizens, in this word of dedication, we wish to express a cordial greeting and, indeed, congratulations. For this radio hour is one of service to America, which certainly will listen in interestedly, and even sympathetically, I am sure, to the voice of the ancient Church with its historic background of all the centuries of the Christian era, and with its own notable contribution to the discovery, exploration, foundation and growth of our glorious country.

Thus to voice before a vast public the Catholic Church is no light task. Our prayers will be with those who have that task in hand. We feel certain that it will have both the good will and the good wishes of the great majority of our countrymen. Surely, there is no true lover of our Country who does not eagerly hope for a less worldly, a less material, and a more spiritual standard among our people.

With good will, with kindness and with Christ-like sympathy for all, this work is inaugurated. So may it continue. So may it be fulfilled. This word of dedication voices, therefore, the hope that this radio hour may serve to make known, to explain with the charity of Christ, our faith, which we love even as we love Christ Himself. May it serve to make better understood that faith as it really is—a light revealing the pathway to heaven: a strength, and a power divine through Christ; pardoning our sins, elevating, consecrating our common every-day duties and joys, bringing not only justice but gladness and peace to our searching and questioning hearts.

Made in the USA
Monee, IL
25 January 2025

10048962R00154

THE CHRIST

THE CHRIST

FULTON J. SHEEN

Addresses Delivered in the Catholic Hour Program
Produced by the National Council of Catholic Men
Sundays of December 27, 1931, to March 27, 1932
Sundays of December 23, 1934, to April 21, 1935
Good Friday, April 19, 1935

✳ ✳ ✳

CLUNY
Providence, Rhode Island

CLUNY EDITION, 2025

This Cluny edition is a compilation of the addresses contained
in *Manifestations of Christ* (1933) and *The Fullness of Christ* (1935),
both originally published by the National Council of Catholic Men.

For more information regarding this title
or any other Cluny Media publication,
please write to info@clunymedia.com, or to
Cluny Media, P.O. Box 1664, Providence, RI 02901

WWW.CLUNYMEDIA.COM

ISBN: 978-1-68595-381-2

IMPRIMATUR:
John Francis Noll, D. D., *Bishop of Fort Wayne*

Cover design by Clarke & Clarke
Cover image: Paolo Veronese, *The Crucifixion*,
circa 1580, oil on canvas
Courtesy of Museum of Fine Arts, Budapest

CONTENTS

THE CHRIST

PART ONE

MANIFESTATIONS OF CHRIST

DEDICATED TO
the Cherished Virgin Mary, Mother of Jesus,
Holy Gateway through which God came to men,
in prayerful supplication and petition that
loving souls seeking Love may find thee:
the Door through which
men pass back again to God

* * *

INTRODUCTION

THESE sermons originally delivered over the Catholic Hour sought to illumine souls concerning Christ and His Church. Now they are set down in printed form in order that they may continue that same apostolic mission. The ear has heard, and now the eye can see. It remains for the heart and soul to embrace. The author will not feel that his work has enjoyed any success, even though its reception be great or its praise high, unless at least a single soul who may have chanced to read it, is lifted up to a better living of that life which is divine, a better understanding of that truth which is the Word, and a deeper love of that love which is the Spirit of God. In a world that is constantly looking for new faiths, new religions, and new creeds, there can be nothing more new or novel than to begin to practise and live the truths of Christianity.

Fulton J. Sheen

MOTHER AND BABE

DELIVERED ON DECEMBER 27, 1931

THIS is Christmas, the season when eyes and hearts are drawn in memory and in love to a Babe who was born in a cave under the floor of the world, and who, by that act, shook the world to its very foundations. It is the season of the stupendous mystery of Omnipotence wrapped in swaddling bands and laid in a manger. Divinity is always where you would least expect to find it. No one in the world would ever have thought of looking for God in the form of a babe. No one in the world would ever have suspected that He who threw the great fiery ball of the sun in the heavens, would one day be warmed by the breath of oxen. No one in the world would ever have suspected that hands which could tumble planets and worlds into space, would be one day smaller than the huge heads of cattle. No one in the world would ever have suspected that He who could make the stars as His canopy would one day be covered by the roof of a stable. And yet such are the ways of God. In order to confound the power of the world He comes in the weakness of a child and in order to set at naught its pride makes His bed in straw. The world He made as His home and yet the world received Him not, and thus Christmas is the story of a God who was homeless at home.

But while we pay this primary act of adoration to the God who brought heaven to earth, there is danger that some of us may forget just how the Child came into the world; in fact, certain modern forms of Christianity speak of the Babe, but never a word about the Mother of the Babe. The Babe of Bethlehem did not fall from the heavens into a bed of straw, but came into this world through the great portals of the flesh. Sons are inseparable from mothers, and mothers inseparable from sons. You cannot go to a statue of a mother holding a babe, and cut away the mother, leaving the babe suspended in mid-air, neither can you cleave away the Mother from the Babe of Bethlehem. He is not suspended mid-air in history, but like all other babes, came into the world by and through His Mother. While we adore the Child, then, should we not venerate His Mother, and while we kneel to Jesus, should we not at least clasp the hand of Mary for giving us such a Savior? There is a grave danger that, lest in celebrating a Christmas without the Mother, we may soon reach a point where we will celebrate Christmas without the Babe. And what an absurdity that would be, for just as there can never be a Christmas without a Christ, so there can never be a Christ without a Mary.

May I, therefore, ask you to go with me and pull aside the curtains of the past, and under the light of Revelation discover the role and interpret the part that Mary played in the great Drama of Redemption?

Almighty God never launches a great work without exceeding preparation. The two greatest works of God are the Creation of the first man, Adam, and the Incarnation of the Son of God, the new Adam, Jesus Christ. But neither of these was accomplished without characteristic divine preparation.

God did not make the masterpiece of creation, which was man, on the very first day, but deferred it until He had labored for six days in ornamenting the universe. From no material thing, but only by the fiat of His will, Omnipotence moved and said to nothingness, "Be," and lo and behold, spheres fell into their orbits, passing one another in beautiful harmony without ever a hitch or a halt. Then came the living things: the herbs bearing fruit as unconscious tribute to their Maker; the trees, with their leafy arms outstretched all day in prayer, and the flowers opening the chalice of their perfumes to their Creator. With the labor that was never exhausting, God then made the sensitive creatures to roam about, either in the watery palaces of the depths, or on wings, to fly through trackless space, or else as unwinged to roam the fields in search of their repast and natural happiness. But all of this beauty, which has inspired the song of poets and the tracings of artists, was not in the divine Mind sufficiently beautiful for the creature whom God would make to be the lord and master of the universe. He would do one thing more: He would set apart, as a choice garden, a small portion of His creation, beautify it with four rivers flowing through lands rich with gold and onyx, permit to roam in it the beasts of the field as domestics of that garden in order to make it a paradise of the most intense happiness and pleasure that was possible on earth. When finally that Eden was made beautiful, as only God knows how to make things beautiful, He launched the masterpiece of His creation: the first man, and in that paradise of pleasure was celebrated the first nuptials of humanity—the union of flesh and flesh of the first man and woman: Adam and Eve.

Now if God so prepared for His first great work, which was man, by making the paradise of Creation, it was even more fitting that before sending His Son to redeem the world, He should prepare for Him a paradise of the Incarnation. And for four thousand years He prepared it by symbols and prophecies. In the language of types He prepared human minds for some understanding of what this new paradise would be. The burning bush of Moses inundated with the glory of God, and conserving, in the midst of its flames, the freshness of its verdure and the perfume of its flowers, was a symbol of a new paradise conserving in the honor of its maternity the very perfume of virginity. The rod of Aaron flourishing in the solitude of the Temple, while isolated from the world by silence and retreat, was a symbol of that paradise which in a place of retirement and isolation from the world would engender the very flower of the human race. The arch of alliance where the Tables of the Law were conserved was a symbol of the new paradise in which the Law in the Person of Christ would take up His very residence.

That paradise was prepared for, not only by symbols, but also by prophecies. Even in that dread day when an angel with a flaming sword was stationed in the first garden in creation, a prophecy was made that the serpent would not eventually conquer, but that a woman would crush its head. Later on Isaias and Jeremias hailed that holy paradise as one which should encircle a Man.

But prophets and symbols were a too distant preparation. God would labor still more on His Paradise. He would make a Paradise not overrun with weeds and thistles, but blooming with every flower of virtue; a Paradise at whose portals sin had never knocked, nor against whose gates infidelity would never dare to storm; a Paradise from which would flow not four rivers through lands rich with gold and onyx, but four oceans of grace to the four corners of the world; a Paradise destined to bring forth the Tree of Life, and therefore full of life and grace itself; a Paradise in which was to be tabernacled Purity itself, and therefore one immaculately pure; a Paradise so beautiful and sublime that the Heavenly Father would not have to blush in sending His Son into it, and that Paradise of the Incarnation to be gardenered by the Adam new, that flesh-girt Paradise in which there was to be celebrated the nuptials, not of man and woman, but of humanity and divinity, is our own beloved Mary, Mother of our Lord and Savior, Jesus Christ.

And thus, as we gather about the crib of Bethlehem, we somehow feel that we are in the presence of a new Paradise of beauty and love and innocence, and that the name of that Paradise is Mary. God labored for six days and produced Eden for the first Adam; now He labored anew, and produced the new Eden, Mary, for the new Adam, Christ. And if we could have been there in that stable on the first Christmas night, we might have seen that Paradise of the Incarnation, but we should not be able to recollect whether her face was beautiful or not, nor should we be able to recall any of her features, for what would have impressed us, and made us forget all else, would have been the lovely sinless soul that shone through her eyes like two celestial suns, that spoke in her mouth which only breathed in prayer, and that was heard in her voice, which was like the hushed song of the angels. If we could have stood at the gates to that Paradise we should have less peered at it, than into it, for what would have impressed us, would not have been any external qualities, though these would have been ravishing, but rather the qualities of her soul—her simplicity, innocence, humility, and above all, her purity—and so completely would all these have taken possession of our soul, as so much divine music, that our first thought would have been, "Oh, so beautiful!"; and our second thought would have been, "Oh, what hateful creatures we are!"

Tell me why should not that Paradise of the Incarnation be spotless and pure? Why should she not be immaculate and stainless? Just suppose that you could have pre-existed your own mother, in much the same way that an artist pre-exists his painting. Furthermore, suppose that you had an infinite power to make your mother anything that you pleased, just as a great artist like Raphael has the power of realizing his artistic ideals. Supposing you had this double power, what kind of mother would you have made for yourself?

Would you have made her of such a type that would make you blush because of her unwomanly and unmotherlike actions? Would you have in any way stained and soiled her with the self-ishness that would make her unattractive not only to you, but to your fellow man? Would you have made her exteriorly and interiorly of such a character as to make you ashamed of her, or would you have made her, so far as human beauty goes, the most beautiful woman in the world; and so far as beauty of soul goes, one who would radiate every virtue, every manner of kindness and charity and loveliness; one who by the purity of her life and her mind and her heart would be an inspiration not only to you, but even to your fellow man, so that all would look up to her as the very incarnation of what is best in motherhood? Now, if you who are an imperfect being and who have not the deli-cate conception of all that is fine in life, would have made the loveliest of mothers, do you think that our blessed Lord who not only pre-existed His own Mother, but who had an infinite power to make her just what He chose, would, in virtue of all the infinite delicacy of His Spirit, make her any less pure and lov-ing and beautiful than you would have made your own mother? If you who hate selfishness, would have made her selfless, and who hate ugliness would have made her beautiful, do you not think that the Son of God who hates sin would make His own Mother sinless, and who hates moral ugliness, would have made her immaculately beautiful?

I plead, therefore, for a Christmas in which the Babe is not an orphan, but a Child of Mary; I plead for a religion which breathes respect for motherhood, and vibrates with a love for that Mother, above all mothers, who brought our Savior into the world. If there is any man or woman looking for a test as to what constitutes the divine religion on this earth, let him apply the same test he would to the judgment of a man. If you ever want to know the real qualities of a man, judge him not by his attitude to the world of commerce, his outlook on business, his kindness and his genteel manners, but judge him rather by his attitude to his own mother. If you want to know the quality of a religion, judge it exactly the same way, that is, not by the way it seeks to please men, but rather by the attitude that it has to the Mother of our blessed Lord. If you find a religion which never speaks of that woman who gave us our Redeemer; which, in its liturgy and its devotions, is silent about the most beautiful of women; which, in its history has even broken her images and statues, then there certainly must be something wanting to the truth of that religion, and let me say, even to its humanity.

Our blessed Lord could hardly be expected to look with favor on those who forgot His Mother, who nourished Him as a babe, carried Him into Egypt, caressed Him as a child, and stood at the bedside of the cross when, with almost His last breath, He tenderly called her "Mother." Really, one of the great inconsistencies of the modern world is its sentimental and almost commercial attachment to "Mother's Day," and its complete forgetfulness of the Mother of mothers, the Mother of our Lord, and the Mother of men, without whom all motherhood is without a Christian ideal. I can understand why a man should love his mother, but I cannot understand why a man who calls himself a Christian and a follower of Christ should not have a very deep and intense love for Christ's Mother. I repeat, therefore, that a quick test for the divinity of any religion is its outlook on the Mother of Christ. And if you want to know just how intense and deep and loyal our love is to that sweet Mother, then place your hands over our hearts.

Christmas takes on a new meaning when the Mother is seen with the Babe. In fact, the heavens and the earth seem almost to exchange places. Years and years ago, aye, centuries ago, we used to think of heaven as "way up there." Then one day the God of the heavens came to this earth, and that hour when she held the Babe in her arms, it became true to say that with her we now "look down" to heaven.

In these days when mother is separated from child, which is birth control, and a husband is separated from his wife, which is divorce, we plead for the return of the ideal Mother and we address her:

With our forlorn and cheerless condition, Sweet Queen, we pray thee, give us patience and endurance. When our spirit is exalted or depressed, when it loses its balance, when it is restless or wayward, when it is sick of what it has and hankers after what it has not, when our mortal frame trembles under the shadow of the tempter, we shall call on thee, and ask thee to bring us back to ourselves, for thou art the cool breath of the immaculate, the fragrance of the rose of Sharon—thou art the Paradise of the Incarnation—thou art the Mother of our Savior—thou art our Queen—our Mother— our Immaculate Mother—and we love thee!

* * *

THE THRILL OF MONOTONY

DELIVERED ON JANUARY 3, 1932

AS another New Year rolls round in the cycle of time, one wonders how many are depressed with the monotony of years. It is an undeniable fact that the world hates the mere fact of repetition just as much as it loves the shock of the new. The modern man hates the monotony of the same wife, and to escape it seeks refuge in divorce. He dislikes exceedingly living according to the morality of the Ten Commandments, and to escape its monotony he develops new morals and prefaces to morals. He dislikes also the monotony of a life that is consecrated to a single purpose, and a final end, and to escape it, often with his own hands, shuffles off his mortal coil. This positive distaste of repetition so characteristic of our day alone explains the constant demand for new thrills, new excitements, new psychologies, new religions, new morals, new gods, new everything to arouse the already jaded sensibilities, and the soul weighed down with the world ennui.

If one asks just why monotony is so distasteful to our age, one is met with this answer: "Everything that is full of life loves change, for the characteristic of life is movement toward a new goal, and urges toward new pleasures. Being essentially directed to novelty, life can never rest in the tediousness of repetition."

This argument has never appealed to thinking men as thoroughly sound. I believe that just the contrary is true, and instead of saying that those who are full of life hate monotony we should say that those who are full of life find a positive thrill in monotony. To prove this point one can appeal to those who are essentially full of life and who, therefore, enjoy the thrill of monotony, namely, a child, God, and His Incarnate Son: our blessed Savior.

First of all, the child. If you place a child upon your knees and bounce it up and down three or four times, the child, full of the passion of life, will cry out, "Do it again." If you tell a child a delightful fairy story, the child will never say, "Oh, that is an old one. I heard Uncle Ray tell that last week," but he will say, "Tell me again." If you are very clever and can blow smoke through your eyes, or even through your ears, the child is never content with just the one trick of magic, but will say, "Do it again." You may build houses of cards, and then tear them down, and feel that you have exhausted your repertoire when you have done it once, but the child is not so easily depressed with repetition, and with joyous appeal will sing out, "Do it again." Simply because the child is full of life, he wants to see things unchanged and to be repeated over and over again, for to his brimming enthusiasm there is inseparably linked the wondrous thrill of monotony. And what is true of the child is true of God, or better perhaps, what is true first of God is true of the child and God—both love repetition.

When on that first great day of creation God saw the first rose unfold its red petaled chalice in tribute to Him, He did not feel that it would be a dull, drab world if roses went on producing roses till the crack of doom, so He did not ask that a rose should be turned into a stone. When He saw the first tree before Him with its great arms outstretched to the heavens as if in supplication, He did not feel that it would be a monotonous world if trees went on reproducing trees until Gabriel sounded his golden trumpet, and so He commanded that every tree and every plant should reproduce itself according to its kind; for repetition is the sign of glowing and throbbing life. When He heard the first shrill notes of the canary, He did not think that the world would be dull and tiresome if canaries went on reproducing canaries and their song even to our own sad days, so He did not ask that a canary be changed into a buttercup.

Because God is full of life, He enjoys the thrill that comes with sameness, and so I can imagine Almighty God with something of the joy and exuberance that belongs to a child, saying every morning to the sun, "Do it again," and every evening saying to the moon and stars, "Do it again," and every springtime saying to the daisies, "Do it again," and every winter saying to the snowflakes chiseled by some great heavenly smith, "Do it again," and every minute saying to the mountain streams, as great silver ribbons, "Do it again," and every time a child is born into the world, to the eternal confusion of birth control, giving a divine curtain call and asking for a divine Encore in order that the heart of a God might once more ring out in the heart of a babe.

It was only natural, then, that when God sent His beloved Son onto this earth that He should teach the lesson that God taught at creation, namely, the gospel of the thrill of monotony. There was ever a beautiful monotony in the story of His life; thirty years obeying—not one year; three years teaching—not one year; three hours redeeming—not one hour. And as He lived He taught, and all His garnered wisdom could be summed up in the words, "Do it again." There was the monotony of sacrifice—"Take up your cross daily, and follow me"; the monotony of kindness—"If one strike thee on thy right cheek, turn to him also the other"; the monotony of mercy—"How often should we forgive? Till seven times? Aye, till seventy times seven times"; the

monotony of birth—"Nicodemus, unless a man be born again…
he cannot enter into the kingdom of God"; the monotony of
sacrificial thoughtfulness—"Do this in commemoration of me";
the monotony of prayer—"And He prayed the third time"; the
monotony of miracles, for St. John tells us that if he recorded all
the miracles our blessed Lord had worked, the world would not
be large enough to contain the books thereof. There was only
one time in His life that He ever cursed a thing, and that was the
day He saw the barren fig tree which was not producing its fruit
in due season, and therefore was not enjoying the thrill of the
monotonous.

But why, it may be asked, is there a thrill in monotony? There
is necessarily bound to be a thrill in working toward any goal or
fixed purpose, and therein is the final reason for the romance
of repetition. There, too, is the line of division between genuine
Christianity and modern paganism. The Christian finds a thrill
in repetition because he has a fixed goal; the modern pagan finds
repetition monotonous because he has never decided for himself the purpose of living. Instead of passing the test, the modern mind changes the test, instead of working toward an ideal,
it changes the ideal; instead of tending repetitiously toward a
fixed point, the modern mind changes its point of view, and
calls it progress. It is no wonder life is dull, when one has not
decided the purpose of life; it is no marvel that existence is drab,
if one has never discussed the reason for existence. How dull, for
example, golf would be if there were never a green; how monotonous a theatre, if there were never a last curtain; how monotonous would be a sea voyage, if there were never a port, or a
journey, if there were never a destination. How insipid poems
would be if there were never a last line, and heaven only knows
how tiresome sermons would be, if there were never a last word;

and so it is with life. Since the modern mind has never decided the goal of life, nor the purpose of living, nor the reason of existing, but like a weather-cock changes with every wind of doctrine and suggestion, it is necessarily bound to find life dull, drab and monotonous.

Contrast this goalless existence with the Christian point of view in which a man has an ultimate end and purpose in life. Do you think, for example, that Dubois, who labored for seven years to make the cast for the statue of Jeanne d'Arc, found his artistic life dull and monotonous? Each day's work, repetitious though it was, brought to him the thrill of seeing the goal of the finished masterpiece come closer and closer. Do you think that the musicians or the scholars who practice and study for days upon days find their work monotonous? To them each repeated moment is just a preparation or a step toward the goal of either a thrilling recital, or a great intellectual discourse. Once admit a purpose in life, and each and every act which tends toward that point, bears the unmistakable stamp of joyfulness and cheer. The Christian has his fixed goal, namely, to make his life more and more Christ-like. His own nature is like a block of marble, and his will is the chisel. He looks out upon his model, Christ, and, with the sharp points of his mortifying chisel, cuts away from his nature huge chunks of cold selfishness, and then by finer and more delicate touches makes the great model appear forthwith, until finally only the brush of a hand is needed to give it its polished finish. There is no man living who has this Christian ideal who believes that repeated acts of faith, hope and charity, prudence, justice, fortitude and love, are tainted with what the modern mind would call monotony. Each new conquest of self is a new thrill, for each repeated act brings closer and closer that love we fall just short of in all love, eternal union with our Lord and Savior.

Sometimes, of course, it is not easy to see just how much progress we are making toward our goal, but though we never see the progress, we never lose sight of the goal. Then we are very much like the tapestry workers, who work not from the front of the tapestry, but from the rear, keeping ever before their eyes the little model to be realized. They go on drawing thread after thread in a monotonous but thrilling way, never destined to see their completed work until the last thread has been drawn, and the tapestry is turned about to show them how well and how truly they have labored.

> *My life is but a weaving*
> *Between my God and me.*
> *I may but choose the colors,*
> *He worketh skillfully.*
> *Full oft He chooses sorrow,*
> *And I, in foolish pride,*
> *Forget He sees the upper,*
> *And I the under, side.*

The Christian, therefore, is always bound to have a great advantage over the modern pagan, simply because he knows where he is going, whereas the modern pagan knows not. The pagan must always be a pessimist, for he must always feel that this life is too short to give a man a chance, and the Christian will always be the optimist, for he knows that this life is long enough to give a man a chance for eternity. That is why the Christian can be joyful. That is why the pagan is sad and depressed.

Picture a child with a ball, and suppose that he is told that it is the only ball he will ever have to play with. The natural psychological reaction of the child will be to be fearful of playing too much with it, or bouncing it too often, or even pricking it full of pin holes, because he will never have another ball. But suppose that the child is told that perhaps next month, perhaps next week, perhaps even in five minutes, he will be given another ball, which will never wear out, which will always give joy, and with which he will never tire of playing. The natural reaction of the child will be to take the first ball a little less seriously, and to begin playing with it joyously and happily, not even caring if someone does prick it full of pin holes, because he is very soon going to have another ball which will endure forever.

The child with one ball is the modern pagan who has only one ball in the sense that he has one sphere, one world, one life, one earth. He cannot enjoy the earth as much as he would like because he must always be fearful of the earth being taken away from him. He can never even tolerate that any suffering or pain should ever come to his little ball, the earth, for it is the only ball that he will ever have to play with. The Christian, on the other hand, is the one who believes that some day, perhaps even tomorrow, he will have another ball, another world, another sphere, another life. And so he can play with this earth, enjoy its monotony and even be resigned to its pin-pricks, for he knows that very soon he is going to have the other ball, which is the other life that shall never wear out nor become tiresome, because its life is the life of the Eternal God, the beginning and the end of all that is.

When, therefore, seized and suffused through and through with the Christian ideal of making Christ shine out in your life, and when in the routine of Christian living you have begun your morning with a prayer and asked the Father's blessing on all your goings and comings; and when you have broken your fast with the Eucharistic Lord at the altar, and knelt in adoration before the uplifted Host and the glowing chalice, and when you have sanctified the day by offering each deed in union with the Master, and sanctified each trial by linking it with the cross, and repressed unkind words and unjust criticisms out of love for Him who prayed for His enemies on the cross, and, when the day is done, you again kneel in thanksgiving and in humble gratitude to the Father of Light, and when after having done this day after day, week after week, and year after year in a constant effort to make your life more Christ-like, and you wonder just what other thing needs to be done to bring you just a step closer to the goal of everlasting peace and happiness, then remember the lesson of the thrill of monotony: "Do it again."

* * *

THE RIGHT OF SANCTUARY

DELIVERED ON JANUARY 10, 1932

IN these days it is almost impossible to call our souls our own, for the psycho-analytic mood has seized us like a pestilential fever. Every sin and failure of a soul, every crime and secret passion of a heart, every unholy falling from a holy purpose is broadcast to a world only too ready to find a justification of its own wrongs in hearing the wrongs of others.

In the face of this condition, the world needs an institution something like that which flourished in the Middle Ages, namely, the Right of Sanctuary. This right was based upon the inviolability attached to sacred things. A fugitive guilty of felony was considered immune from prosecution by law, provided he entered the sanctuary of a church. The principle behind this right was that any criminal who entered the sanctuary had equivalently cast his lot with God, and therefore was immune, for a certain period of time, from the searchings of men.

The world today needs just some such haven of rest where we might be alone with ourselves and our God, and not have our sins published to the world; some place of shelter from the curious eyes of those who would not bind up our wounds, but delight in our anguish; some solitary harbor where we might escape those who ask us to reveal, but who never stop to heal; some sanctuary where our sins would not be told to the world, nor allowed to fester unseen within our heart. And the world has such a sanctuary which respects the inviolability of the human person, wherein a soul may cast its lot not upon inquiring men but upon a forgiving God, and that is the Sacrament of Penance, which, by figure of speech, is referred to familiarly as Confession.

What does confession demand? It demands two things: a confessor and a penitent, and only God could find both. First of all, it demands a confessor; a man who will look kindly on the denying Peters, speak words of forgiveness to penitent Magdalenes, breathe words of comradeship to betraying Judases; a man with intensity of love for his work, and with universality of love for his penitents; a man signed with the sign and sealed with the seal of Christ; one who has a heart of fire for charity and a heart of bronze for chastity; a man with discretion, that is, with a mind strange to curiosity, vanity and fear; and finally, a man with a heart like an immense well into which sins, like stones, may be dropped, but a well so deep that no sound comes back from those depths to an ear which might be bent to hear.

But immediately I hear it said: "But why should I confess my sins to a man; for the priest is a man? Why should I not tell them directly to God? Why should a confessor stand between my God and me?"

Is it asking too much that you confess yourself to someone who has been constituted a delegate of divine justice and divine mercy? Is it asking too much that God should send out ambassadors to deal with those who have broken off relations with Him? At the present time, for example, diplomatic relations are broken off between Russia and America. America, therefore, never deals through direct diplomatic channels with the Soviet government.

If she has any dealings with the Soviets, it is through a third party. Is it not just, therefore, that since man by sin has broken off diplomatic relations with God, that he, therefore, should deal with God through the intermediary of His ambassadors? Why should we admit this to be just in one case, in the case of human government, and deny it to be just in the case of divine government? And, as a matter of fact, does not God deal with our fellow men through ambassadors in other walks of life? The source of all law is God, and the presidents and kings and parliaments throughout the world, in the administration of law, are really acting in His name. God has even given to heads of governments the power of taking away life. If, therefore, some men share God's justice by punishing, why should not others share God's mercy by forgiveness? It is the very order of life that we should have the doctor for our body, the teacher for our mind, the president for our government—why, then, should we not have confessors for our souls?

Confession demands not only a confessor, but also a penitent, and here too the wisdom of God is supremely revealed. The penitent must be created by God as the confessor was created by God. Making a penitent means taking a man in his pride, and the icy silence which envelops the avenues of his soul, and saying to him: "You shall come, and kneel at the feet of a man who, in his human estate, may be no better than you are, but who is nevertheless an ambassador of Christ, and to that man you shall reveal that which you hide from your friends and relatives, that which makes you blush when alone, that which you lock in the storehouse of your memory; and, as you confess these secrets on bended knees, you shall say to that man: 'Father, forgive me, for I have sinned.'"

Hard though it is, this narration of sins by a penitent answers a need of the human heart. How often history reveals that a guilty man, pressed by conscience alone, and driven on by some mysterious influence stronger even than conservation of life, will make him refuse the immunity which silence promises, and force him to avow the very sin which will bring the punishment he sought to avoid. In moments when man has feared neither witnesses nor tortures, he has cried out: "Yes, it is I! I did it." There is something even in the most hardened criminal at times which makes him give himself up to justice, by an avowal of his guilt in order that he might have peace of mind.

Just as a foreign substance like a piece of glass which is taken into the body is gradually thrown off by the body; and just as a poison taken into the stomach irritates it until the stomach finally throws it off, so, too, the heart of man, irritated and weary by the poison of sin, seeks the catharsis of spirit by which it too may pour its wrong and the poison of its sins into the ear of a friend.

And even those who have no great crimes upon their souls, but are weighted down by a heart which seems not right with God, crave some confidant to whom they can unpack their hearts with words. In joy and in sorrow, every heart needs someone who will suspend his own preoccupations to listen to its own, and who will drop all his cares to take in the burden of its own. The most unfortunate mortals are those who shed their tears in silence because there is no one to wipe them away. How many men and women there are in the world who, through sin, have felt themselves alone, cast off from everyone, and who in their inmost heart have felt the need of some sanctuary into which they might retire for consolation and direction! Our cities are full of souls who are constantly crying out, "What can I do?" and to these and the millions who are yearning for someone who will understand and pardon as Christ understood and pardoned the Penitent Thief, the confessional is the answer.

If the world had never known the Sacrament of Penance, and someone proposed instituting it, there would be a universal cry from all men saying that "humanity is too proud" and hence there will never be penitents. "Humanity is too indiscreet" and hence there will never be confessors. But the fact—here I speak as a priest—that the world comes to our feet, children of seven years and their elders of seventy, hearts of sixteen years, hearts of sixty years; the fact that there comes the mother with her daughter, the father with his son, the precious desires of youth with the chagrins of old age, the innocent souls who never lost baptismal grace, and the great prodigals who lost it and found again the fountains of mercy, and the fact that all these tell us that which the ear of a spouse does not hear, nor the ear of a brother know, nor the ear of a friend suspect, proves and proclaims to the world that there are penitents because there are confessors, and there are confessors because there are penitents, and there are both because Jesus Christ is God.

There is no institution in the world so effectively working for social reform as the Church through the confessional, and this for the double reason that the confessional gets at the intention which inspires the act, and reforms the group by reforming the individual which makes it up.

The Church, in the confessional, after the manner of her divine Founder, proceeds on the principle that if it is wrong to do a certain thing, it is wrong to think about that thing. She does not wait until the desire or the intention passes into act; rather she goes into the very confines of a conscience and lays her finger on the desire to sin and brands it as a sin, even though the desire is never realized. Mindful of the words of our blessed Lord she does not wait until a man actually commits adultery, but she holds that any man commits adultery even if he lusteth after a woman in his own heart. She demands that the defaulting cashier confess his intention to steal money, even though he finds it impossible to do so. She holds, as against modern morality, that it is too late to legislate when the act has been done; it is too late to pass a law when you have to call a policeman; it is too late to really heal when you have to establish fact-finding commissions. The facts of crime, drunkenness, and social evils are merely the putting into action of base thoughts, intentions and desires, and the Church in insisting that every illicit motive and every evil desire be confessed, is getting at the hidden springs and roots of action, and in keeping them clean she keeps actions clean; by making man pure on the inside, she makes man pure on the outside, and by making him right with God, she makes him right with his fellow man.

The Church in the confessional is, furthermore, the only institution in the world today that reforms society by reforming the individual who makes it up. Modern social reform begins with the group and ends with the individual; the Church in the confessional begins with the individual and ends with the group. Modern morality talks about crime, which is a group problem; the Church in the confessional talks to the criminal, who is the individual problem. Modern morality talks in the abstract about the problem of drunkenness; the Church in the confessional talks in the concrete to the drunkard and asks him not to psycho-analyze his mental state for sublimation, but to reveal his moral state for purgation. And of these two methods, the confessional is the only really effective one, for just as the only way to make a family good and happy is to make each individual in the family happy, so, too, the only way to make society peaceful is to make each individual citizen peaceful, and this cannot be done except by making each conscience right with its God. Modern morality is in a tower shouting to rebellious soldiers below; the Church, through her officers, is mingling with the soldiers individually, bidding each one to submit to law which is, in the last analysis, the ordinance of God. Thus it is that by making individual adjustments, and by treating each conscience singly, and judging it not by the way it makes for worldly success, but by the way it is ordered to God, the confessional purifies each individual stream and river that runs into the *great* social ocean, and if that ocean today does not seem clean and bright, it is only because there are some streams that have not been made clean at their source by the distilling and refining pardon of God's great Sacrament of Mercy.

If, therefore, our government and our social reformers are really sincere about the betterment of society, they must begin to recognize the importance of intention and the importance of the individual; they must more and more see that we cannot allow citizens to think badly and expect them to act rightly, nor can we expect a commission to legislate morality for a nation, without, in some way, seeing that each individual in the nation is himself moral and righteous with his God. We will not be made a moral nation by permitting our educators to tell us there is no such thing as sin, nor shall we be made a righteous nation by permitting reformers to emphasize sin to the point of morbidity. There is only one way to have the fact of sin, and not to have the fact of its overemphasis which is morbidity, and that is through the confessional which tells a man that he is a sinner, but also tells him that he can, by God's pardon and grace, become a saint.

There is a fable about a man being locked in a little box, and when the box was opened it was found that he had the heart of a giant. That box is the confessional box, and the heart of the priest is the heart of a giant, and from the heart of that giant there come the consoling words of Christ: "Come to me, all you that labor and are burdened, and I will refresh you." And the penitents who hear those words then begin to understand the tremendous paradox of God's pardon—if we had never sinned, we never could call Christ "Savior."

* * *

THE ONLY THING
THAT MATTERS

DELIVERED ON JANUARY 17, 1932

THE utterly disillusioned man, uprooted from the past and disinherited by tradition, is wandering about the modern Babylon, and like a man who knows not where he is going, pictures to himself a thousand destinations. He seeks refuge in a humanistic outlook, and takes pride in the progress of civilization, and yet down in his heart knows that he is confusing comfort with civilization and change with progress. He needs an infusion of new blood; he needs the cross, fertilization with eternity, and to help him discover himself, we here set down the Catholic philosophy of life in which are indicated the stepping-stones to those great peaks. The steps are threefold, one following the other in logical fashion: first, silence; second, reflection; and third, primacy of the spiritual.

Silence
One of the really great needs of our own day is silence. Modern life seems to thrive on a fondness for noise, and by noise I mean not only the staccato barbarism of jazz, or the bleating and moaning of saxophone orchestras, but also, and principally, the desire for that which distracts: love of amusements, constant goings and comings, excitements, and thrills, and movement for the mere sake of movement. What is the reason of this fondness for noise? It is not due to any inherent love of that which is loud, for people generally prefer that which is soft and refined. Rather

the reason is to be found in the great desire on the part of human beings to do the impossible, namely to escape from themselves. They do not like to be with themselves, because they are not pleased with themselves; they do not like to be alone with their conscience, because their conscience reproves and carries on an unbearable repartee. They do not like to be quiet, because the footsteps of the Hound of Heaven can be heard in silence, but cannot be heard in the din of excitement; they do not like to be silent, because God's voice is like a whisper and it cannot be heard in the tumult of the city streets. These are some of the reasons why the modern world loves noise, and they are all resolvable to this: they drown God's voice and stupefy conscience. The result is that very few people ever know themselves. In fact, they know everyone else better than they know themselves. That is why so few ever see their own faults.

In order to remedy this condition, what is needed is less amusing and more musing; a silence; a going apart into the desert of our souls to rest a while; a solitariness from men and an aloneness with God; a quiet which permits the soul to be sensitive to the whispers of God; a requiem or a rest from modern maxims and the excuse of new philosophies and the excitements which appeal to the body and disturb the soul; a privacy inspired by the example of Him who, least of all mankind, needed a preparation of silence for a life of activity and yet had the greatest of them all; a tranquility inspired by Him who in the midst of a busy life spent whole nights on mountain tops in prayer.

In order to attain this requiem and silence it is not necessary to travel to the quiet of the oriental skies, for silence is not dependent upon a place, but upon a state of mind. It is not based on where we are but what we are thinking about. It is being alone, so far as the world is concerned, even though one is in the very midst of it—an activity by which every faculty of the heart and mind and soul is bent inward, awaiting the voice of God.

Reflection

Silence constitutes the environment of the second effect of entering into ourselves, namely, reflection. In moments of silence, men begin to seek God. The soul begins to part company with animal desires, and begins at least a blundering search for the hiding place of that haunting presence which seems to speak to them from every burning bush. The embryonic instinct for heaven now cries out for its object, and as the vague sense of unexplained powers conditions it, reflection begins, and reflection means asking oneself the question, "Why am I here?" and finding the answer in the words of the penny catechism: "To know, love and serve God on this earth, and be happy with Him forever in the next."

Suppose I stopped a clerk, a banker, a merchant, a messenger-boy, on the way to work tomorrow morning, and suppose I put to each the question, "Whither are you going?" He would answer, "To my labor." "But, why do you labor?" "I labor to earn a reward." "But suppose I told you that a very wealthy man had died and left an immense fortune to all who labor; would you be interested in knowing the conditions upon which that fortune might be yours?"

There is not one who would refuse. And yet, Almighty God has Himself promised a heavenly reward to all men who labor. Why are they not interested in learning something of its conditions? Why are they not concerned in discovering the ways and means to its possession? If we are concerned with an earthly reward, why should we not be concerned with a heavenly reward? If we are concerned with a temporal livelihood, why should we not be concerned with an eternal life? What, after all, is the use of amassing wealth, if God is going to require our soul? Our shrouds will have no pockets. Was not this the point in the parable of the man who filled his barns? He added store to store, building to building, and in our own language, dollar to dollar, and then said to his soul, "Soul, thou hast much goods laid up for many years, take thy rest; eat, drink, make good cheer." But God said to him, "Thou fool, this night do they require thy soul of thee: and whose shall those things be which thou hast provided?" "So is he that layeth up treasure for himself, and is not rich towards God." Reflection on such a parable convinces the soul that the great idea, after all, is not the question which is so often asked by the modern world on the occasion of a death, "What did he leave behind?" but rather, "What did he take with him?" For it is only good works that follow.

The answer to the question of destiny is that I have been made to know, love and serve God for all eternity. Just as there are heavenly bodies which can complete their orbits only after the lapse of ages, and which then reappear with unfailing precision at the point from which they started, as if to present themselves once more to Him who sent them on their way, so, too, each soul that is sent into this world from that great white throne of God, to run its course over a brief span of years, is destined to reappear once again before Him who sent it on its way, freighted with virtues and loaded with the precious cargo of merits to receive the crown He made for us the day of our birth.

Primacy of the Spiritual

After silence, and the reflection that God is the end of all and the only peace and rest for souls, there comes the sudden and certain recognition of the primacy of the spiritual, which is the essence of the true Christian life. The primacy of the spiritual means that there is nothing in the world that really matters except the salvation of our soul, and that in its salvation the spiritual must reign over the temporal, the soul over the body, grace over nature, and God over the world. Religion means this or it means nothing. This was the great emphasis of our Lord Himself, and it therefore cannot be any less the emphasis of anything Christian. Had we been on the mountainside of Capharnaum some twenty centuries ago, mingled with the shepherd and fisherman audience of Galilee; had we felt the upland breath of that autumn evening on whose wings the great Teacher's accents rose and died away; had we marked the eyes of Jesus, invited by the note of a bird's whirling overhead, or caught by the beauty of a distant lily floating in the Lake of Galilee, or as He pointed to the pastures brilliant with gold amaryllis, and heard the praise of the flowers that toil not; had we seen Him point to the green grass which carpets the mountainside, and heard Him draw from all the other beauties of nature lessons that Heaven tells, we should have learned that the very stars above our heads were less mysteries than the creatures below, and we should have been ashamed of our want of trust and providence in Him who made us.

One great and tremendous thought would disengage itself from His sermon on that occasion, namely, the supremacy of the world of the spirit: "Lay not up for yourselves treasures on earth: where the rust and moth consume, and where thieves break through, and steal. But lay up to yourselves treasures in heaven… Behold the birds of the air…consider the ravens…for they neither sow, nor do they reap, nor gather into barns: and your heavenly Father feedeth them. Are not you of much more value than they? And which of you, by taking thought, can add to his stature one cubit? … If then ye be not able to do so much as the least thing, why are you solicitous for the rest? ... And for raiment why are you solicitous? Consider the lilies of the field, how they grow: they labor not, neither do they spin. But I say to you, that not even Solomon in all his glory was arrayed as one of these. And if the grass of the field which is today and tomorrow is cast into the oven, God doth so clothe: how much more you. Oh, ye of little faith! Be not solicitous therefore, saying: 'What shall we eat, and what shall we drink, or wherewith shall we be clothed?' ... And be not lifted up on high... For after all these things do the heathens seek. For your Father knoweth that you have need of all these things. But seek ye first the kingdom of God, and His justice, and all these things shall be added unto you."

The Church is the only institution in the world today which is emphasizing the spiritual above all things else. That is why she scandalizes the world. That is why the pagans hate her. And despite the hate she reasserts that nothing matters in life but the salvation of a soul. That is why she builds her schools in order that children may never grow up without hearing the name of God, and bowing their knees to their Lord and Savior. That is why she has marriage laws and insists that the faith of the Catholic party and the children born of the marriage be safeguarded; that is why she holds that if a state would command a violation of the law of God, the individual must die rather than disobey his Creator.

Consonant with this ideal, the Church holds that a tiny child who knows the existence of God and believes in the Trinity, knows far more, and is better entitled to a University degree, than professors scattered throughout the length and breadth of this land who do not know that beyond time is the Timeless, and beyond space is the Spaceless, the Infinite Lord and Master of the universe.

The Church believes, furthermore, that a holy hour spent before the Blessed Sacrament does more good for the well-being of the world than whole days spent in talking about progress to the utter oblivion of the fact that the only true progress consists in the diminution of the traces of original sin; she believes that a penitent returning to God is of far more consequence than the cancellation of war debts; that an increase of sanctifying grace in a soul is of far more value than the increase of international credit; that a group of cloistered nuns in prayer are more effective in preserving world peace than a group of world politicians discussing peace to the forgetfulness of the Prince of Peace; that all the beauties of nature do not compare in the smallest degree with the beauty of a soul in the state of grace; that the profoundest of scientific discoveries is as naught compared with the superior intellectual intuitions of a child at its first Communion; that the success of world policy based on the Christian principle of justice would be a great force for the salvation of millions of men; that it really does not matter very much whether children ever confuse Aristides with Aristotle, but it does matter if they confuse Buddha with Christ; that the fact that millions listen to a preacher over the radio is of no importance whatever compared with the visit of one soul to hear the sweet whisperings of Jesus from the tabernacle; that poverty is not the greatest curse; that physical infirmity is not the greatest ill; that the loss of a member of a family is not so serious as the loss of faith; that all the kingdoms of earth are as the least grain in the balance compared to a kingdom of a human heart where Mary is Queen and Christ is King.

Is this excessive? Is this a loss of a sense of proportion? Is this foolishness? If it is, it is the foolishness of our Lord: "What doth it profit a man if he gain the whole world and suffer the loss of his own soul."

Every devotion to a heavenly ideal must seem foolish to a world whose ideals are of the earth earthly. To some minds it must have seemed foolish for our Lord on the Mount of Temptation to have repulsed Satan, when Satan, in a wild orgy of triumphant pride revealed in all their fugitive splendor the great procession of the kingdoms of earth, and promised them to the Lord if only falling down He would adore him.

The foolishness of the divine Founder has been the foolishness of the divine Church. She, too, is set high on the mountain top of the world. To that mountain, as to the Mount of Temptation, the spectres of false progress, new freedom and worldly success come to her, and in vision remind her of all the sects which would join her communion, all the individuals which would join her ranks, and of all the opposition, and persecution of the world that would cease if only falling down she would adore worldly success, be a little less interested in the spiritual education of the young, a little less emphatic about the sanctity of marriage, and a little less concerned with the salvation of souls.

With the quickness of a lightning flash the Church, conscious of fellowship with her divine Master, echoes back the words of her Master, the charter cry of spiritual freedom: "Seek ye first the kingdom of God and His Justice."

And as the spectre of error and worldly success makes its way down the mountain top, it finds at its base all the little kingdoms of passing theories and ephemeral faiths prostrate in sickening adoration before it, and in contrast to the great kingdom set high upon the mountain, the spectre of worldly success, like the spectre of Satan, begins to realize and understand that the greatness of the world never tempts the great—but only the small!

THE FREEDOM OF AUTHORITY

DELIVERED ON JANUARY 24, 1932

STEVENSON once said that not on bread alone doth man live, but principally on catchwords. High-sounding phrases often go rattling by like express trains, carrying the burden of those who are unable to think for themselves. Among these phrases or catchwords there is none in the field of religion which has greater modern appeal than the one: "The modern man wants a religion of the spirit, and not a religion of authority." Years ago its popular expression was that "we must be free from the slavery of Rome." Today it is more direct: "No Catholic can be free because he is bound down by law and authority."

In order to clarify the teachings of the Church concerning authority, law and freedom, we shall here develop the two following propositions: First, obedience to highest law and authority constitute freedom; second, the obedience to the law and authority of the Church is thrilling and romantic.

Our blessed Lord once said that the Truth would make us free. By this He meant that only by obedience to the highest law and authority do we become free. To take an example from the realm of arts. If an artist in a fever of broad-mindedness and a desire to be free, chooses to paint a giraffe with a short neck, he will soon discover that he will not be free to paint a giraffe at all. If in a feverish love for the new art of self-expression which obeys no law, he decides to paint a zebra without stripes, and a leopard without spots, and a triangle with four sides, he will soon discover that he is not free at all to paint even zebras, leopards or triangles. It is only obedience to law and authority and the inherent nature of things that we ever become free.

Another example in the field of science: Imagine a railroad steam engine endowed with consciousness, so that it is able to read, to think, to speak. And supposing that one day it picked up with its pilot one of the modern books on the morality of self-expression, such as one of Mr. Bertrand Russell's, in which he rebels against obedience to traditional moral laws, and the authority of Christian teaching. And suppose, with its great single Cyclops eye, it reads the pages of this liberal thinker, and becomes so impressed with his fine sophistic idioms that it whistles to itself: "Mr. Russell is right. What do the engineers who designed me, and imposed their laws upon me know about my inner impulses? Why should I even obey the authority of an engineer who is constantly limiting my steam pressure to one hundred pounds a square inch, when I have the vital Freudian urge to make it one hundred and fifty pounds? And, furthermore, why should I submit myself to the authority of railroad officials who, fifty years ago, laid the tracks upon which I should run? Why should I take this curve, that straightaway, this bridge, simply because they decided over two score years ago that I should? Why should I not be permitted to choose my own directions, and to make my own tracks? From now on, I am going to be self-expressive!"

Well, suppose the steam engine did become self-expressive. It would soon learn two things: first, in refusing to obey the laws concerning steam pressure, it would discover it was no longer free to be a steam engine, because in asserting its pressure beyond the normal, it would burst its entrails; second, by refusing to keep on the track it would no longer be free to run. And if the steam engine did jump the track, and burst its boilers, it would not hurt the engineer who designed the track; it would hurt only the engine itself. And so, too, if a man disobeys God's laws, and dashes his head against them, as against an eternal rock, the rock does not suffer—it is only the head of the man that suffers.

Finally, it is only by obedience to the laws of Christ and His Church that we ever become free. If there is any vision or mental picture to be had at all of the condition of the world a few centuries ago and now, it might be the vision of a great rocky island in the very center of a stormy and raging sea. Previously to the break-up of Christian unity three centuries ago, this island may be represented as surrounded by a great stone wall against which the waves spent their fury, but never broke it down. Inside the wall were thousands and thousands of the children of God playing games, singing songs, and enjoying life, to the utter oblivion of the great devouring sea outside. With the dawning of the day of false freedom, there came to the island a group of men who argued with the children in some such language as this: "Why have you permitted the Church of Rome to surround you with all her laws and dogmas? Can you not see that she has surrounded you all about, and has not permitted you to think for yourself or to be free and captains of your own fate? Tear down the walls, break down the barriers, throw off the obstacles, and begin to live your own life, and learn to be free." And so the children tore down the walls; and one day I went back and I saw all the children huddled together in the center of the island, afraid to move, afraid to play, afraid to sing, afraid to dance, afraid to be gay, afraid of falling into the sea.

We who, by the grace of God, have been blessed with the protection of the Church's law and authority, can never quite understand why anyone can ever think that obedience to that law and authority is enslaving. On the contrary, to us it is positively romantic. It is easy to fall into the excesses of the modern world, to talk about progress, new thought, new religion, just as it easy to fall off a log.

It is easy to be an atheist, and to say the world does not require a God, just as it is easy to be a pantheist, and say that the world is God; but it is thrilling to walk between those two abysses and hold that God is in the world, but not of it—and such is the Incarnation. It would be extremely easy to fall into the extreme of the Stoics, and say that pain is the law of life, or to fall into the equally stupid extreme of saying pleasure is the law of life, but it is romantic to escape the pitfalls and hold that pain is the prelude to life—and such is the lesson of Easter.

It would be easy to say with Gandhi that life should be a fast, just as it would be easy to say with the pagan that it should be a feast, but it is thrilling to avoid both extremes, and hold that the fast should precede the feast. Every heresy in the history of the Church has been either a truth exaggerated to an excess, or diminished to a defect. It is easy to fall into any of these extremes, and to lose one's intellectual balance. The thrill is in keeping it.

In other words, the Church is not so much to be compared with Niagara Falls, as it is to be compared with a great and tremendous rock weighing ten thousand tons, which is poised on another rock by the delicate balance of no more than six inches of a base. Niagara is a falls simply because it cannot help falling; it is the easiest thing to do; it is simply letting things go. But that great rock which is pitched at an angle no bigger than one's hand has a thousand angles at which it will fall, but there is only one on which it will stand, and it is that which makes it a far more serious thing, than the falling and churning of all of Niagara's waters. And so with the Church. All through her history she has been like that great rock, poised on the very brink of an abyss, and it is that which has made her romantic; for danger is the root and foundation of all romance in drama.

Why do children like to play robber, walk picket fences, tramp into thick woods, play along banks of deep rivers, throw stones at vicious dogs, listen to blood-curdling ghost stories, walk on roofs? Is it not because each and every child has deep-rooted in his heart as the foundation for his manhood, and as the very condition for his enjoying life, the love of danger and the thrill of being near it, and yet never falling completely into it?

Why has every person an instinctive desire to witness a storm at sea, providing he could be sure of reaching port? Is it not because there is romance in escaping danger? We who ride in Peter's bark witness such a storm, and know we will reach port. For twenty centuries the bark of Peter has been riding the seas, and for twenty centuries we who have been on board know the romance of the seas and its dangers, but also the romance of a port. Sometimes that bark has come within a hair's breadth of dashing against the rock of saying that Christ was man and not God, and then again it has suddenly had to swerve to avoid crashing into the opposite rock and saying that Christ is God but not man. At other moments in her voyage, Peter's bark has come within a razor's edge of being stranded on the sands of humanism and saying that man does everything, and God does nothing. And then, by an equally dexterous move, she saves herself from the sandbars of declaring with the oriental mystics that God does everything and man does nothing. It would have been extremely easy for Peter and his successors to have sunk their ship in the depths of determinism in the last century, just as it would have been easy for it to have capsized in the shallow waters of sentimentalism in the twentieth century. But it is wonderfully thrilling to have avoided both. It would have been very easy for the bark of Peter to have been lost in the fogs of modernism in our own day, just as it would have been easy for it to have lost its course in the mists of Freudian sexology. But to have avoided both of these snares, not by mere chance, but by intelligent direction, is thrilling. If one small blunder concerning the doctrine of original sin were made in her twenty centuries of charting the course of men to God, huge blunders would have been made in human happiness. A mistranslation of a single word one thousand years ago might have smashed all the statues of Europe. A false move in the Council of the Vatican might have impoverished reason. By one single slip, the Church might have stopped all the dances, withered all the Christmas trees, and broken all the Easter eggs.

But the Church has avoided all these pitfalls and all these errors, and as the bark of Peter, with sails flying high, cuts the waters of the sea, she looks before and aft. Behind her she can see the shriveled hulks of a thousand heresies and mental fashions that were dashed to pieces against the rocks of time; she can see ten thousand shallow basins into which she might have plunged, and ten thousand rivers of sentimentalism in which she might have been drowned. Now the bark of Peter is in the open, with the sea calm and clear, but there are shouts about her ears. Every now and then she stops to gather up shipwrecked children from the sinking rafts of sinking faiths, then onward she speeds, and the future will be just as thrilling as the past. Always in danger, always escaping it; always threatened, always conquering; always enjoying the romance of avoiding extremes, the bark is destined to go on through all the storms and tempests of the world, until one day it checks pace at the hid battlements of eternity, and there as the children disembark from the ship of Peter, they will understand why it avoided the snares and pitfalls—because as Peter stood at the helm of his bark, there rested on his hands the invisible, eternal hands of Christ, who steers the sun and moon and stars in their courses.

* * *

THE WORLD'S GREATEST NEED

DELIVERED ON JANUARY 31, 1932

THERE is a famine abroad on the earth, a famine not of bread, for we have had too much of that and our luxury has made us forget God; a famine not of gold, for the glitter of so much of that has blinded us to the meaning of the twinkle of the stars; but a famine of a more serious kind, and one which threatens nearly every country in the world—the famine of really great men. In other words, the world today is suffering from a terrible nemesis of mediocrity. We are dying of ordinariness; we are perishing from our pettiness. The world's greatest need is great men, someone who will understand that there is no greater conquest than victory over oneself; someone who will realize that real worth is achieved, not so much by activity, as by silence; someone who will seek first the Kingdom of God and His justice, and put into actual practice the law that it is only by dying to the life of the body that we ever live to the life of the spirit; someone who will brave the taunts of a Good Friday to win the joy of an Easter Sunday; who will, like a lightning-flash, burn away the bonds of feeble interest which tie down our energies to the world; who, with a fearless voice, like John the Baptist, will arouse our enfeebled nature out of the sleek dream of unheroic repose; who will gain victories, not by stepping down from the cross and compromising with the world, but who will suffer in order to conquer the world. In a word, what we need are saints, for saints are the truly great men.

Now, we cannot all become saints, in the strictest sense of the term, but we can all become saints to a certain degree, and

42

THE CHRIST

I am going to try to explain in simple psychological terms how saints are made. I assume without further ado that the grace of God is the one thing necessary, and that God will give that grace to those who do His will. I am concerned merely with the natural elements of sanctity, or the psychological steps which lead to the state of sainthood, and these are three: a sense of emptiness, a knowledge, and an exchange.

First of all, I say that they are made by an experience of the emptiness of the world, and its absolute incapacity to give peace and happiness to the human heart. Consult your own experience. When you were children you looked forward to Christmas Day, and in anticipation you imagined all the joys that would be yours with the possession of your toys, the sight of the lighted tree, and the unlimited taste of fruits and candies. When finally Christmas Day did come, and you had played with the toys (and it was not long until you were "played out"), and you had tasted the sweet meats and blown out the last candle on the tree, you then crept into your bed, and said in your own little heart of hearts that somehow or other, it did not come up to your expectations. It did not, for nothing does. That experience of childhood has been repeated a thousand times since. Men look forward to the possession of power; they finally get it, and still they are unhappy. Men crave wealth, they have a hundred times more than they need, and still they want more; and their wanting it makes them unhappy. Even the loss of the least of it robs them of joy, as the plucking of a single hair from a head that is full of it, gives pain. Nothing ever comes up to our expectations!

Well, why is it? The reason is that in looking forward to the things of this world, we use our imagination, which, as a faculty of the soul is spiritual, and therefore capable of imagining

43

infinite things. I can imagine, for example, a mountain of gold, but I have never seen one. I can imagine a castle on the Hudson that has a thousand times a thousand rooms, each wall blazing with diamonds and emeralds, but I have never seen that castle, and perhaps never shall.

Now, the pleasure of the future, the joys which I hope to obtain, the power which I desire to wield, the wealth which I desire to possess—all of these, as long as they are not actually in my possession, become endowed with the infinity which belongs to the imagination. They, in a certain sense, become spiritualized and idealized, and hence take on something of the blessedness and infinity of my imagination. But when finally these imaginings or expectations are realized, they are material, they are local, definite, concrete, finite, cribbed, confined. In the mind they were ideal, and hence almost unbounded; in reality, they are concrete, and therefore very limited. Hence there arises a tremendous disparity between the infinite imagination I had of these things and the finite realization. When the things actually do come, they come with a sense of loss. We feel that in their becoming actual or real, they lose something of the beauty with which we had imaginatively endowed them. A sense of emptiness or void then comes over the soul. We feel that we have been cheated out of something, for the realization of our imagination is like trying to fill a valley with a pea; a terrible sense of emptiness creeps over the soul, and this sense of void is really a call from God. In very simple terms, it means that we cannot expect happiness here below. It means that we are made for an infinite happiness, otherwise we never could have imagined it. But it also means that we can never obtain it here below, for otherwise we should never have this terrible feeling of loss, and disappointment, and emptiness.

Two escapes are possible from this feeling of emptiness and dissatisfaction of the world, or better still, from the voice of God. One is to drown the call of God by seeking new pleasures, new stimuli, new excitements. Some souls use the remedy and go on chasing butterflies and golden pots at the end of the rainbow, and throw themselves into pleasures that satisfy a very small part of themselves, and never their whole being. Others let loose the reins of duty upon the flanks of the steeds of passion, and gallop on down the avenues of pleasures, always being made more hungry by that which satisfies, until at last despair drives them to suicide and double death.

Saintly souls, on the other hand, when they feel this sense of uneasiness in their soul, conclude that happiness is not to be found on this earth, that they were made for God, and that the only unhappiness in life is the unhappiness that comes from a failure to tend towards Him. At this point begins the second stage of the development of great men, namely, a knowledge (and by knowledge I mean an understanding) of our Lord and Savior. Let me here again appeal to your personal experience. You may have heard a great deal about a certain person, about his mannerisms, his severity, his rigorous life. You only know about him, but you do not know him. With this meager knowledge, you frankly avow that you do not care for him. After spending five minutes in his company, your whole feeling has completely changed. Knowledge changed your whole outlook on him, and converted hate into the beginning of love. In much the same way that the prejudice of Nathaniel against our blessed Lord was changed by just two sentences from our Lord's lips, which swept away prejudice, so it is with the soul of a great man before our Lord. At a distance, He seems to be a crowned king, and the crown is not gold but thorns; He seems to be wearing the garment of a fool, and therefore He is to be spurned; he seems to be holding a reed in His hand, and therefore is only a mock King. But it is only *seems*, for the more we get to know Him, the less we find we can get along without Him. On closer view, we see that He is a King, but not of this world; that the scars are not relics of defeat, but the scars of love in the battle of Calvary. That which we mistook for hardness was devotion to truth; that which we believed to be severity we see was devotion to love— and so the process goes on, until we find that in comparison to His beauty, all other beauty is pain, and in comparison to His love, all earthly love is but tawdry and vain.

At this point begins the third stage of sainthood, namely, exchange. There is a wrong impression abroad in the world to the effect that following our Lord means giving up the world, abandoning friends, surrendering wealth, and losing all that life holds dear. If we fear that in having Him we must have naught else besides, we have not begun to understand Christ.

Such is not really the case. Sanctity is not a question of relinquishing or abandoning or giving up something for Christ: it is a question of exchange.

Our Lord never said it was wrong to love the world; He said only that it was a loss, for "what exchange shall a man give for his soul?" Exchange is founded on the fact that there are two classes of goods: first, things that we can get along without; second, things we cannot get along without. I can very well get along without a dime, but I cannot get along without the bread which it will buy, and so I exchange one for the other. So, too, in the spiritual world, I soon learn that there are many things that I can get along without, and as I grow in acquaintance with Christ, I find that I can get along without sin, but I cannot get along without His peace of conscience, and so I exchange one for the other.

Later on, as I get to know Him better, I find that I can get along without an innocent pleasure, but I cannot get along without the pleasure of daily communion with Him, and so I exchange the one for the other. I find by a still deeper acquaintance that I can get along without the world's goods, but not without the wealth of Christ's grace, and so I exchange one for the other, and that is the vow of poverty. I find that I can get along very well without the pleasures of the flesh, but I cannot get along without the pleasures of Christ's spirit, and I exchange the one for the other, and that is the vow of chastity. I find that I can get along very well without my own will, but I cannot get along without His, and so I exchange the one for the other, and that is the vow of obedience. Thus the saint goes on exchanging one thing for another. And thus it is that in making himself poor, he becomes rich, and in making himself a slave, he becomes free. The gravitation of the earth grows weaker, and the gravitation of the stars grows stronger, until finally, when there is nothing left to exchange, like Paul he cries out: "For to me…to die is gain," for by that last exchange his gain is Christ in everlasting life.

Sanctity, then, is not giving up the world. It is exchanging the world. It is a continuation of that sublime transaction of the Incarnation in which Christ said to man: "You give me your humanity, I will give you my divinity. You give me your time, I will give you my eternity. You give me your bonds, I will give you my freedom. You give me your death, I will give you my life. You give me your nothingness, I will give you my all." And the consoling thought throughout this whole transforming process is that it does not require much time to make us saints: it requires only much love.

And now, in exchange for telling you how saints are made, kindly give me your prayers, that I may practice what I preach.

THE DIVINE SENSE OF HUMOR

DELIVERED ON FEBRUARY 7, 1932

A remark not to be taken too lightly is one to the effect that the modern world is taking itself too seriously. Whether there be only five senses or fifty-seven senses, one of the most precious of them all is the one the modern world is rapidly losing, namely, the sense of humor. There are many evidences to justify the statement that the world is losing its sense of humor. Note, first of all, the changed attitude toward laughter. It was not so long ago that laughter was as free as the air, and as spontaneous as a sneeze, being the natural product of human fellowship, and the joyous effervescence of friend meeting friend. Now it is put on a commercial basis, and the business of making people laugh has become one of the serious enterprises of our country; in fact, so serious has it become that we are now obliged to pay about two dollars for an evening of it in a theatre.

Gold, too, is taken so seriously today that some men pursue it as if it were the "be all and the end all here" and as if shrouds had pockets and coffins had coffers. If it is lost, some feel that life is no longer worth living, as if life consisted in what we *had* rather than in who we *are.* Another evidence is the seriousness with which the modern world embraces every new fad and fancy in the intellectual order, simply because it is new. The only real explanation for the craze over every new psychology that lost its soul, then its consciousness, and now has lost its mind, and the only real explanation for the equally absurd theory that everything wrong in life is traceable to a sex libido, is that the modern world has lost its sense of humor. If these absurd theories about God being a creature of space-time, and religion being, as one philosopher puts it, "a projection into the roaring loom of time of a unified complex of psychical values," were advanced fifty years ago, people would have laughed them out of existence. The only reason the modern world holds them is that it has lost its appreciation of what is funny, it has lost its sense of humor.

It might be interesting to inquire into the history of the sense of humor, and this is best studied in relationship to this visible world of ours. In order that we might more clearly grasp its history, we ask ourselves three questions: When did humor come into the world? When did the world lose its sense of humor? How did it regain it?

The Origin of the Divine Sense of Humor

There never was a brush touched to canvas, nor a chisel to marble, nor a dome thrown against the vault of heaven's blue, but that a great idea preceded it, for all art is the expression of the ideal through the real. The architect, for example, who conceived the Cathedral of Notre Dame, had an idea of that cathedral in his mind before a single stone of it was put upon stone. Had he lived to see his work completed, he would have seen in that stone tribute to the Blessed Mother, the realization, the consecration, or the petrification of his idea.

Now Creation is an art—the divine Art of the divine Artist. Everything that exists in this world, every stone, every diamond, every plant, every tree, every animal, every bird, every man, every child was made according to a divine idea existing in the mind of God from all eternity. God, too, had His "models" or "patterns" and these were the "archetypal ideas" or things which were identical with His very Being. When, therefore, the divine

Fiat spoke to nothingness, and planets and worlds tumbled from God's fingertips, and the great procession of life moved on, everything which existed either in the most distant planet, or on our tiny earth, was a realization, or a materialization, or an incarnation of His ideas.

Almighty God willed that just as any great painting should make us think of the artist, and every great monument should remind us of the architect who designed it, and every painting recall the painter and every machine the inventor, so, too, everything in this world should, in some way, remind us of Him. In other words, God made the world with a *divine sense of humor.*

But what has this to do with a divine sense of humor? Do we not say that a person has a sense of humor if he can "see through things," and do we not say that a person lacks a sense of humor if he cannot "see through things?" But God made the world according to such a plan that we were constantly to be "seeing through things" to Him, the power, the wisdom, the beauty and the source of all that is. In other words, the material was to be a revelation of the spiritual, the human the revelation of the divine, the fleeting and the passing the revelation of the Eternal. The universe, according to His original plan, was transparent, like a window pane, and in those days a mountain was not just a mountain; a mountain was the revelation of the power of God; a sunset was not just a sunset; a sunset was the revelation of the beauty of God; a snow-flake was not just a snow-flake; a snow-flake was the revelation of the purity of God. Everything told us something about God, for by the visible things of the world is the power and wisdom of the invisible God made manifest. According to this plan, every man was a poet, for a poet is one who is endowed with this sense of the invisible, the power of seeing God through things, and such is the essence of humor.

The Loss of the Sense of Humor

Such was God's plan of Creation, or rather its great drama, perfect in detail without flaw or blemish. But the drama, with each line exquisitely sketched by God, was given to man to act and to play, and man made a botch of the masterpiece. That one thing which destroyed man's plan in Creation, though not God's plan, was sin, and sin is seriousness. Sin is an act by which man refuses to use creatures as a stepping-stone to God, or as a means to an end, and insists on using them as ends in themselves. As a man loses his sense of humor when he cannot see through a point, so, too, he loses his sense of humor in its entirety when he ceases to see things in revelations, or symbols, or reminders of God, and begins to regard them seriously as ends in themselves. The day sin came into the world, the world lost its transparency, and became opaque, like a curtain. A veil was drawn between the Artist and His artistry, between the Architect and the architecture, between the Creator and the creation. The sense of the invisible was lost. In his mental short-sightedness, man lost the power "to see God through things": then a mountain was just a mountain; a sunset was just a sunset; a snow-flake was just a snow-flake. Poetry passed out of the world, and prose came in—prose, which is a matter-of-factness of style—and men settled down to that terrible seriousness in life which must always characterize those who cannot see beyond the veil.

Rebirth of the Sense of Humor

This seriousness pervaded the world for full forty centuries. Then one night there rang out over the stillness of an evening breeze the cry of the heart of a God in the voice of a child. And when the Babe grew in grace and wisdom, He went into the public lanes and marketplaces, and began to teach a new doctrine to men—the doctrine of the divine sense of humor. Everything He said, everything He did could be summed up in these words: *Nothing in this world is to be taken seriously, nothing*—except the salvation of a soul. "For what doth it profit a man if he gain the whole world, and suffer the loss of his own soul." The world, and the things that are in it, will one day, like an Arab's tent, be folded away. There is nothing that endures but God.

And so, as He went about preaching, He taught the lesson of the divine sense of humor and never took anything seriously except His soul. He saw the fishermen gathering in their nets, but He did not take them seriously. To Him they were fishers of men. The pearl was not to be taken seriously, for thanks to the divine sense of humor, the pearl was the worth of faith and grace. The quickness of the lightning-flash from east to west was not just a physical phenomenon to be taken seriously. To Him it was the revelation of the quickness of judgment. A wedding garment was not to be taken seriously—though June brides do take it seriously—a wedding garment was a revelation of charity. And so on, all through His life. Every material thing He viewed as a tell-tale of some great eternal lesson. Every trivial incident was a symbol of God's working among men. The fishes of the sea, the birds of the air that reap not nor sow, the lilies of the field arrayed in garments more glorious than Solomon's, camels and eyes of needles, gardens and husbandmen, thorns and thistles, bread and serpents, sheep and goats, wheat and chaff, hen and chickens, and all other parables of His ministry—all these seemingly insignificant things of ordinary life were to Him as transparent as the very air, and each and every one of them contained within itself a wonderful lesson about the goodness of God, but only those who had a divine sense of humor and who could see through things as He did, could read the lesson. The serious can never speak in parables, but only those with a sense of the invisible.

Such is the history of the divine sense of humor, and now that we know what it is, we may ask who are they who understand and possess it, and here the answer must be that those who possess it in its fulness are saints.

I do not mean canonized saints, but rather that great army of staunch and solid Christians to whom everything and every incident speaks a story of God's love. A saint can be defined as one who has a divine sense of humor, for a saint never takes this world seriously as the lasting city. To him the world is like a scaffolding up through which souls climb to the Kingdom of Heaven, and when the last soul shall have climbed up through it, then it shall be torn down and burned with a fervent fire, not because it is base, but simply because it has done its work—it has brought souls back again to God. A saint is one who looks out upon this world as a nursery to the Father's heavenly mansion and a stepping-stone to the Kingdom of Heaven. A saint is one to whom everything in the world is a sacrament. In the strict sense of the term, there are only seven sacraments, but in the broad sense of the term everything in the world is a sacrament, for everything in the world can be used as a means of special sanctification. A saint is one who never complains about the particular duty of his state in life, for he knows full well that "all the world's a stage, and all the men and women merely players." Why, then, should he who plays the part of a king glory in his tinsel crown and tin sword, and believe that he is better than someone else who plays the part of a peasant? For when the curtain goes down they are all men. So, too, why should anyone, who in this world happens to enjoy either the accident of honor or wealth, believe he is better than someone else who may possess neither gold nor worldly learning? Why should he glory in his tinseled crown and tin sword, and believe that he is better than someone else who plays a less important role in the great drama of life? For when the curtain goes down on the last day, and we respond to the curtain call of judgment, we shall not be asked what part we played, but how well we played the part that was assigned to us.

A saint, then, is one who has learned to spiritualize and sacramentalize and ennoble everything in the world, and make of it a prayer. No occupation is too base for such spiritualization, nor is any suffering too hard for such ennobling. It is only those who have not this highly developed sense that let the opportunities of daily life pass by without either making of them a prayer, or taking from them a divine lesson. Centuries ago in the streets of Florence there stood a beautiful piece of Carrara marble that had been cut and hacked and ruined by some cheap artist. Other mediocre artists passed it by, and bemoaned that it should have been so ruined. One day—so a story runs—Michaelangelo passed it by, asked that it be brought to his studio, there applied his chisel, his genius and his inspiration, and drew out of it the immortal statue of David. The lesson contained herein is that there is nothing so base or low that it cannot be reconquered, that there is no duty, however menial, that cannot be retrieved for sanctity, and that there is nothing that is cast down that cannot be lifted up.

Down in the gutter of a city street was a drop of water, soiled, dirty and stagnant. Away up in the heavens a gentle sunbeam saw it, leaped out of its azure sky down to the drop, kissed it, thrilled it through and through with new strange life and hope, and lifted it up higher and higher and higher, beyond the clouds, and one day left it as a flake of immaculate snow on a mountain top. And so our own lives—humdrum, routine, tiresome lives of a workaday world—can be ennobled, spiritualized and sacramentalized, providing we bring to them the inspiration of Someone who saw apostolic zeal in salt; provided we infuse their carbon blackness with the electric flame of love which will make them glow with the brilliance of a diamond; provided we bring to them the inspiration of the great Captain, who carried five wounds in the forefront of battle and thrills them with the fixed flash of that instant and intolerable enlightenment, the lightning made eternal as the Light.

And when we have done this, then perhaps we shall understand why He who came to this earth to teach us the divine sense of humor showed us everything that was lovely and beautiful in His character—except one thing. He showed us His power; He showed us His wisdom; He showed us His melting kindness; He showed us His sorrow; He showed us His tears; He showed us His forgiveness; He showed us His power over nature; He showed us His knowledge of human hearts; but there was one thing that He did not show; there was one thing He saved for those who do not take this world too seriously; there was one thing He saved for Paradise; there was one thing He saved for those who, like poets and saints, have a divine sense of humor; there was one thing He saved for heaven that will make heaven heaven, and that was—His smile!

THE CURSE OF
BROAD-MINDEDNESS

DELIVERED ON FEBRUARY 14, 1932

"THE Catholic Church is intolerant!" That simple thought, like a yellow-fever sign, is supposed to be the one solid reason to frighten away anyone who might be contemplating knocking at the portals for entrance, begging a crumb of the Bread of Life. When proof for this statement is asked, it is retorted that the Church is intolerant because of its self-complacency and smug satisfaction as the unique interpreter of the thoughts of Christ. Its narrow-mindedness is revealed in its unwillingness to co-operate effectively with other Christian bodies which are working for the union of churches. Within the last ten years, two great world conferences on religion have been held, in which every great religion except the Catholic participated. The Catholic Church was invited to attend to discuss the two important subjects of doctrine and ministry, but she refused.

That is not all! Even in our own country she has refused to lend a helping hand in the federating of churches, a federation which decided that it was better to throw dogmatic differences into the background in order to serve better the religious needs of America. The other churches will give her a royal welcome, but she will not come. She will not co-operate! She will not conform! And she will not conform because she is too narrow-minded and intolerant. Christ would not have acted that way!

Such is, practically everyone will admit, a fair statement of the attitude the modern world bears toward the Church. The charge of intolerance is not new. It was once directed against our blessed Lord Himself.

Immediately after His betrayal, our blessed Lord was summoned before a religious body for the first Church conference of Christian times, held, not in the city of Lausanne or Stockholm, but in Jerusalem. The meeting was presided over by Annas, primate and head of one of the most aggressive families of the patriarchate, a man wise with the deluding wisdom of three score and ten years, a man wise in a country where age and wisdom were synonymous. Five of his sons in succession wore the sacred ephod of blue and purple and scarlet, symbols of family power. As head of his own house, Annas had charge of family revenues, and from a non-biblical source we learn that part of the family fortune was invested in trades connected with the Temple. The stalls for the sale of bird and beast and material for sacrifice were known as the booths of the sons of Annas. One expects a high tone when a priest goes into business; but Annas was a Sadducee, and since he did not believe in a future life, he made the most of life while he had it. There was always one incident he remembered about his Temple business, and that was the day our Lord flung tables down its front steps, as if they were lumber, and with cords banished the money-handlers like rubbish before the wind.

That incident flashed before his mind now, when he saw standing before him the Woodworker of Nazareth. The eyes of Jesus and Annas met, and the first world conference on religion opened. Annas, ironically feigning surprise at the sight of the Prisoner whom multitudes followed the week before, opened the meeting by asking Jesus to make plain two important religious matters, the two that were discussed later on in Lausanne and Geneva and Stockholm, namely, the question of His doctrine and the question of His ministry. Our Lord was asked by a religious man, a religious leader, a religious authority, a representative of the common faith of a nation, to enter into discussion, to sit down to a conference on the all-important questions of religion, ministry and discipline, and He refused. And the world's first church conference was a failure!

He refused in words which left no doubt in the mind of Annas that the doctrine which He preached was the one which He would now uphold in religious conference, namely, His divinity. With words cut like the facets of a diamond, with sentences as uncompromising as a two-edged sword, He answered Annas: "I have spoken openly to the world…and in secret I have spoken nothing. Why askest thou me? Ask them who have heard what I spoke unto them: behold they know what things I have said."

In so many words Jesus said to Annas: "You imply by your questioning that I am not divine; that I am just the same as the other rabbis going up and down the countryside; that I am another one of Israel's prophets, and at the most, only a man. I know that you would welcome me to your heart if I would say that I am only human. But no! I have spoken openly to the world. I have declared my divinity. I say unto you, I have exercised the right of divinity, for I have forgiven sins; I have left my body and blood for posterity, and rather than deny its reality, I have lost those who followed me, who were scandalized at my words. It was only last night that I told Philip that the Father and I were One, and that I will ask my Father to send the Spirit of Truth to the Church I have founded on Peter, a Church which shall endure to the end of time.

"Ask those who have heard me; they will tell you what things I have said. I have no other doctrine than that which I declared when I drove your dove-hucksters out of the Temple, and declared it to be my Father's House; that which I have preached, that which angels declared at my birth, that which I revealed on Thabor, that which I now declare before you, namely, my divinity. And if this is your first principle, namely, I am not divine, I am just human like yourself, then there is nothing in common between us. So, 'Why askest thou me to discuss doctrine and ministry with you?'"

Some brute standing nearby, feeling himself the humiliation of the high priest at such an uncompromising response, struck our blessed Lord across the face with a mailed fist, drawing out of Him two things: blood, and a soft answer: "If I have spoken evil, give testimony of the evil; but if well, why smitest thou me?" That soldier of the court of Annas has gone down in history as the representative of that group who feel an intense hatred against divinity, but who never clothe it in intellectual language, but in violence alone.

All that happens in the life of Christ happens in the life of the Church. Here in the courtroom of Annas I find the reason for the Catholic Church's attitude in refusing to take part in movements for federation such as those inspired by present world conferences on religion. Happy the Church is that there should be a desire for the union of Christendom, but she cannot take part in any such conference. In so many words the Church says to those who invite her: "Why askest thou me about my doctrine and my ministry? Ask them that have heard me. I have spoken openly through the centuries, declaring myself the Spouse of Christ, founded on the Rock of Peter. Ask those who have heard me. Centuries before prophets of modern religions arose, I spoke my divinity at Nicea and Constantinople. I spoke it in the cathedrals of the Middle Ages; I speak it today in every pulpit and church throughout the world. I know that you will welcome me to your conferences if I say that I am not divine; I know ritualists throughout the world feel the need of my ceremonials, and would grasp my hand if I would but relinquish my claim to be divine. I know a recent writer has argued that the great organization of the Church could be the framework for the union of all Christendom, if I would give up my claims to be the Truth; I know the church doors of the world would rejoice to see me pass in. I know your welcome would be sincere. I know you desire the union of Christendom—but I cannot! Why do you ask me? If your first principle is that I am not divine, but just a human organization like your own, that I am a human institution like all other human institutions founded by erring men and erring women; if your first principle is that I am human, not divine, then there is no common ground for conference. I must refuse."

Call this intolerance, yes! That is just what it is—the intolerance of divinity. It is the claim to uniqueness that brought the blow of the soldier; it is the claim to uniqueness that brings the blow of the world's disapproval. It is well to remember that there was one thing in the life of Christ that brought His death, and that was the intolerance of His claim to be divine. He was tolerant about where He slept and what He ate; He was tolerant about shortcomings in His fish-smelling Apostles; He was tolerant of those who nailed Him to the cross; but He was absolutely intolerant about His statement that those who believe not in Him shall be condemned. There was not much tolerance about His statement that anyone who would prefer his own father or mother to Him was not worthy of being His disciple. There was not much tolerance of the world's opinion in giving His blessing to those whom the world would hate and revile. Tolerance to His mind was not always good, nor was intolerance always evil.

There is no other subject on which the average mind is so much confused as the subject of tolerance and intolerance. Tolerance is always supposed to be desirable because taken to be synonymous with broad-mindedness. Intolerance is always supposed to be undesirable, because taken to be synonymous with narrow-mindedness. This is not true, for tolerance and intolerance apply to two different things. Intolerance applies only to principles, never to persons. Tolerance applies only to persons, never to principles. We must be tolerant to persons because they are human; we must be intolerant about principles because they are divine. We must be tolerant to the erring, because ignorance may have led them astray; but we must be intolerant to the error, because truth is not our making but God's. Hence, the Church in her history, due to reparation made, has always welcomed the heretic back into the treasury of her souls, but never his heresy into the treasury of her wisdom.

The Church, like our blessed Lord, advocates charity to all persons who disagree with her by word or by violence. Even those who, in the strictest sense of the term, are bigots, are to be treated with the utmost kindness. They really do not hate the Church; they hate only what they mistakenly believe to be the Church. If I believed all the lies that are told about the Church, if I gave credence to all the foul stories told about her priesthood and the Papacy, if I had been brought up on lies about her teachings and her sacraments, I should probably hate the Church a thousand times more than they do.

Keeping the distinction well in mind between persons and principles, cast a hurried glance over the general religious conditions of our country. America, it is commonly said, is suffering from intolerance. While there is much want of charity to our fellow citizens, I believe it is truer to say that America is not suffering so much from intolerance as it is suffering from a false kind of tolerance: the tolerance of right and wrong, truth and error, virtue and vice, Christ and chaos! The man, in our country, who can make up his mind and hold to certain truths with all the fervor of his soul, is called narrow-minded, whereas the man who cannot make up his mind is called broad-minded. And now this false broad-mindedness, or tolerance of truth and error, has carried many minds so far that they say one religion is just as good as another, or that because one contradicts another, therefore, there is no such thing as religion. This is just like concluding that because, in the days of Columbus, some said the world was round, and others said it was flat, therefore there is no world at all. Open-mindedness is all right to a certain extent, but if the mind is open all around... Well?

Certainly it should be reasonably expected that religion should have its authoritative spokesmen, just as well as science. If you had wounded the palm of your hand, you would not call in a florist; if you broke the spring of your watch, you would not ask an artisian well expert to repair it; if your child had swallowed a nickel, you would not call in a collector of internal revenue; if you wished to determine the authenticity of an alleged Rembrandt, you would not summon a house painter. If you insist that only a plumber should mend your pipes, and not an organ tuner; if you demand a doctor shall take care of your body, and not a musician, then why should not we demand that a man who tells about God and religion at least should say his prayers?

The remedy for this broad-mindedness is intolerance, not intolerance of persons, for of them we must be tolerant regardless of the views they may hold, but intolerance of principles. A bridge builder of the enemy, and he who is broad-minded on the bridge; the gardener must be intolerant about the weeds of his garden; the property owner must be intolerant about his claims to property; the soldier must be intolerant about his country, as against that of the enemy, and he who is broad-minded on the battlefield is a coward and a traitor. The doctor must be intolerant about disease in his patients, as the professor must be intolerant about error in his pupils. So, too, the Church, founded on the intolerance of divinity, must be equally intolerant about the truths commissioned to her. There are to be no one fisted battles, no half-drawn swords, no divided loves, no equalizing Christ and Buddha in a broad sweep of sophomoric tolerance or broad-mindedness, for as our blessed Lord has put it: "He that is not with me, is against me."

There is only one answer to the problem of the constituents of water, namely, two atoms of hydrogen and one of oxygen. There is only one answer to the question of what is the capital of the United States. There is only one true answer to the problem of two times two. Suppose that certain mathematicians in various parts of this country taught diverse kinds of multiplication tables. One taught that two times two equaled five, another two times two equaled six, another two times two equaled seven and one-fourth, another two times two equaled nine and four-fifths. Then suppose that someone decided it would be better to be broad-minded, and to work together and sacrifice their particular solutions for the sake of harmony. The result would be a Federation of Mathematicians, compromising, possibly, on the pooled solution that two times two equaled five and seven-eights. Outside this federation is another group which holds that two times two equals four. They refuse to enter the federation unless the mathematicians agree to accept this as the true and unique solution. The broad-minded group in conference taunt them, saying: "You are too intolerant and narrow-minded. You smack of the dead past. They believed that in the Dark Ages."

Now this is precisely the attitude of the Church on the subject of the world conference on religion. She holds that just as truth is one in geography, in chemistry and in mathematics, so too, there is one truth in religion, and if we are intolerant about the truth that two times two equals four, then we should be intolerant also about those principles on which are hinged the only really important thing in the world, namely, the salvation of our immortal soul. If the assumption is that there is no divinity, no oneness of truth, but only opinion, probability and compromise, then the Church must refrain from participation. Any conference on religion, therefore, which starts from the assumption that there is no such thing as truth, and that contrary and contradictory sects may be united in a federation of broad-mindedness, must never expect the Church to join or co-operate.

As we grew from childhood to adolescence, the one thing that probably did most to wreck our faith in Santa Claus—I know it did mine—was to find a Santa Claus in every department store window. If there were only one Santa Claus, and he was at the North Pole, how could there be one in every shop window and at every street corner? That same mentality which led us to seek truth in unity should lead us to identically the same conclusion in religious matters.

The world may charge the Church with intolerance, for the world is right! The Church is intolerant, intolerant about truth, intolerant about principles, intolerant about divinity, just as our blessed Lord was intolerant about His divinity. The other religions may change their principles, and they do change them, because their principles are man-made. Religion is not a sum of beliefs that we would like, but the sum of beliefs God has given. The world may disagree with the Church, but the world knows very definitely with what it is disagreeing. In the future, as in the past, the Church will be intolerant about the sanctity of marriage, for what God has joined together no man shall put asunder; she will be intolerant about her creed, and ready to die for it, for she fears not those who kill the body, but rather those who have the power of casting both body and soul into hell. She will be intolerant about her infallibility, for, "Behold," says Christ, "I am with you all days, even to the consummation of the world." And while she is intolerant even to blood in adhering to the truths given her by her divine Founder, she will be tolerant to those who say she is intolerant, for the same divine Founder has taught her to say: "Father, forgive them, for they know not what they do."

There are only two positions to take concerning truth, and both of them had their hearing centuries ago in the courtroom of Solomon, where two women claimed a babe. A babe is like truth: it is one; it is organic; it cannot be divided. The real mother of the babe would accept no compromise. She was intolerant about her claim. She must have the whole babe, or nothing...the intolerance of motherhood. But the false mother was tolerant. She was willing to compromise. She was willing to divide the babe—and the babe would have died of broad-mindedness!

RELIGION WITHOUT DOGMAS

DELIVERED ON FEBRUARY 21, 1932

THE modern man wants a religion without dogmas. Religion, he says, must be free from dogmas which have fettered and hampered thinking for centuries. Religious experience, individual needs, mystic imagination—all these must take the place of outworn creeds. The Catholic Church, in developing dogmas and piling belief on belief, has made itself too complex, has departed from the beautiful simplicity of the Sermon on the Mount. Our blessed Lord, it is further argued, never intended that there should be any iron-clad dogmas, nor that His religion should become overgrown with them.

The only way to determine whether our blessed Lord intended that His religion should have dogmas, or that it should be a matter of vague religious experience, is to go back to His very life, and particularly to the end of it, when He was on trial in a certain courtroom the night before His death. The presiding official in that court was Caiphas, a low type in a high place, the type that finds in religion not a conviction, but a career. At the central point of the inner circumference of a semi-circle he sat—president of the court; at right and left were seated his colleagues. At each end was a clerk, the one to record votes for his acquittal, the other to record votes for his conviction. Some of the members that night were sure to have been only half awake, but Caiphas was thoroughly alert.

No charge of condemnation could be brought against our Lord as long as contradictory statements were made. As soon as one said anything against Him, Sacred Scripture tells us, another contradicted, and a great tumult broke out. One can imagine the charges: one said, "He calls Himself a King," and another contradicted, "No, He does not say that; He only allows others to call Him a King." Another shouted out, "No, as soon as they wanted to proclaim Him a King, He fled away." Some said that He had cured them, but others testified that disease broke out after the cure, and therefore His cure was done by magic. Some said that Jesus and His Apostles did not offer sacrifice in the Temple, while others replied that it was not so. Some tried to prove that Christ and His followers did not celebrate the Passover, but witnesses who were in the Cenacle and had helped to prepare it the day before denied this. One of the Evangelists records in detail the charge: "This man said, 'I will destroy this Temple made with hands, and within three days I will make another not made with hands.'" But another contradicted him, saying: "No, He did not say that: He said that He would build a new Temple." And so the disputes went on. The contradictions caused great commotion. Nothing that was said could give any color of justice to the sentence of death. When order was restored, Caiphas, infuriated by the way matters were going, rose up from the divan and came forward to the very edge of the dais. If witnesses had failed to condemn, Christ Himself must furnish the grounds for condemnation. So, turning to the Prisoner, the false-hearted judge addressed Him: "Answerest thou nothing to the things which these witness against thee?" But Jesus held His peace.

These silences of Jesus were weighty with magnetic eloquence. He did not speak, but looked about Him, with His great calm eyes, at the troubled and convulsed faces of His assassins, and for all eternity judged those phantom judges. In a flash every one of them was weighed and condemned by that look which went straight to their souls. The cheeks of the old man became red with anger at the silence.

"Well, if He will not speak, then He must be forced to speak and voice His own destruction." Caiphas again rose from the seat at the head of the assembly, and with all the authority that could be crowded into words, asked a question that really mattered; a question that did not center about human affairs; a question that called for an answer, as no other question ever asked since the beginning of time called for an answer; a question that required not one of those vacuous, meaningless answers of timid politicians, but an answer clear-cut like chiseled marble, and the question rang out through the assembly: "I adjure thee by the living God, that thou tell us if thou be the Christ, the Son of God." Priests and rabbis, Scribes and Pharisees, learned men of Israel, knew what the question meant. "Art thou the God foretold by prophets, who should come to this world as God, the Savior?" Everyone sprang to his feet, clawing fingers stretching out towards Him.

Jesus hesitated a moment before dazzling those bleared eyes with the splendor of His formidable secret. A terrible, ominous silence settled over the hall that was made the more intense by its contrast with the sound of the distant crowing of a cock, then came the answer: "Thou hast said it: I am! Nevertheless, I say to you hereafter you shall see the Son of Man sitting on the right hand of the power of God, and coming in the clouds of heaven."

He had given a categorical, straight-forward answer about His divinity; He defined Himself; He enunciated a truth, a cold truth, an authoritative principle. *He enunciated a dogma!*

A gleam of satisfaction lighted up the face of Caiphas. He almost sighed a sigh of relief. At last! At last, he had triumphed. His breast was heaving high with the joy of victory. In the shrill voice of an old man, he shouted out: "He hath blasphemed; what further need have we of witnesses?" Drawing out a small knife from under his girdle, and pretending a shocked horror which he did not feel, he rent his priestly garments, tore them top to bottom, letting the torn pieces hang like glorious symbols of a victorious battle. Then member after member of the Sanhedrin rent their garments, and the cloaked ghosts felt themselves relieved of an immense weight. "Behold, now you have heard the blasphemy, what think you?" And all the noisy kennel bayed out their answer: "He is guilty of death." Guilty of death? Yes! He was too dogmatic.

Now let us suppose that, in answer to that question of Caiphas about His divinity and His divine Sonship, our blessed Lord had said: "Far be it from me, Caiphas, to impose any dogmas concerning my divinity either upon you or upon posterity. I do not wish to cramp your spiritual freedom by harnessing you with the dogma that I am the Son of God. Religion must be free from dogmas, and the religious experience of each individual must decide whether I am God, or just a mere man." If, I say, He had made such a statement, do you think He would have been condemned by Caiphas? If he had been what the modern world calls broad-minded, do you think Caiphas would ever have delivered Him over to Pilate? If He had been less dogmatic, do you think He ever would have been condemned? If He had not been so dogmatic about His divinity, He never would have seen the cross.

Before the unbelieving world rends its garments in holy horror of dogmas, let it pause for a moment to hear the reasoned answer of the Church to the charge of dogmatism. First of all, in direct contradiction of many a modern preachment, the Church holds that it is impossible to have a religion without dogmas. To say that one must have a religion without dogmas is to assert a dogma, and a dogma that needs tremendously more justification than any dogma of the Church. What is a dogma? A dogma is an idea, and in this sense a man without dogmas may be said to be a man without an idea. Dogmas there must be as long as there is sound thinking.

History, mathematics, geography, and science all have their dogmas, their abstract principles, and their ideas. That the World War ended on Armistice Day, 1918, is a dogma of history; that Albany is the capital of the State of New York is a dogma of geography; that the sum of the angles of a triangle is equal to two right-angles is a dogma of geometry; that water is made up of two atoms of hydrogen and one of oxygen is a dogma of science. These are luminous truths, sound ideas in various fields of knowledge. Now truths like these in the religious field are called dogmas in the strict sense of the term. That there are three Persons in One God, that Christ is the Son of God, that faith is a gift, that grace is a participation in the nature of God, that the Church is the continuation of the Incarnation—these are dogmas of religion.

Now to ask that religion be free from dogmas is like asking a body to be freed from its backbone, or art to be freed from shapes and proportions, or literature to be freed from grammar. I know there are thousands of minds weak enough to succumb to the succulent abstraction of the sweet catchword, "I believe in religion, but not in theology," but it is only a catchword. Such a mind might just as well say, "I believe in chemicals, but not in chemistry," or, "I believe in health, but not in all the medical dogmas about digestion, vitamins, and assimilation." It is all as vain and as senseless as saying: "I want to be really scientific but let us do away with laboratories and technique."

The only difference between the dogmas of religion and the dogmas of science is that the latter are grounded upon the authority of fallible men, while the dogmas of the Church are grounded upon the authority of God revealing. The religious problem is not whether religion shall be free from dogmas or not, because by the mere fact that a man thinks he creates dogmas. The real problem is which dogmas are we going to accept, those of hearsay, private wish, and the latest catchword of the day, or the funded intelligence of an august line of philosophers, saints and mystics. For the life of me, I cannot see why anyone should accept the authority of the Book of Darwin, and not accept the authority of the Book of Isaiah, nor how anyone can accept the authority of the latest sex theory emanating from Vienna, and not accept the authority of twenty centuries of Christian tradition; nor how anyone can accept the authority of H. G. Wells and not accept the authority of Jesus Christ.

The modern man must decide for himself whether he is going to have a religion with thought, or a religion without it. He already knows that thoughtless politics lead to the ruin of society, and he may begin to suspect that thoughtless religion ends in confusion worse confounded. The problem is simple. The modern man has two maps before him: one the map of sentimental religion, the other the map of dogmatic religion. The first is very simple. It has been constructed only in the last few years by a topographer who has just gone into the business of map-making, and is extremely adverse to explicit directions. He believes that each man should find his own way and not have his liberty taken away by dogmatic directions. The other map is much more complicated, and full of dogmatic detail. It has been made by topographers that have been over every inch of the road for centuries, and know each detour and each pitfall.

It has explicit directions and dogmas such as, "Do not take this road; it is rocky," or, "Follow this road; although rough and rocky at first, it leads to a smooth road on a mountain top." The simple map is very easy to read, but those who are guided by it are generally lost in a swamp of mushy sentimentalism. The other map takes a little more scrutiny, but it is more simple in the end, for it takes you up through the rocky road of the world's scorn to the everlasting hills, where is seated the Original Map-Maker, the only One who ever has associated rest with learning: "Learn of me, and find rest for your souls."

It is the very nature of man to generate children of his brain in the shape of thoughts, and as he piles up thought on thought, truth on truth, doctrine on doctrine, conviction on conviction, and dogma on dogma, in a very coherent and orderly fashion, so as to produce a system complex as a body, and yet one and harmonious, he becomes more and more human; he becomes more and more man. When, however, in response to false cries for progress, he lops off dogmas, breaks with the memory of his forefathers, denies intellectual parentage, pleads for a religion without dogmas, substitutes mistiness for mystery, mistakes sentiment for sediment, he is sinking back slowly, surely and inevitably into the senselessness of stones and into the irresponsible unconsciousness of weeds. Grass is broad-minded. Cabbages have heads, but they have no dogmas.

PILATE AND PATRIOTISM

DELIVERED ON FEBRUARY 28, 1932

ONE issue which will always hold interest is the conflict between Church and State. If one were to set down in some order the objections against the Church on the part of the modern State, they might resolve themselves into these three: first, the Church is perverting the nation by its parochial school system, which embodies a different educational policy than the public school, and by her marriage legislation which admits of no divorce—now the generally accepted thing in society; second, the Church refuses to give tribute to America, inasmuch as her heart is across the sea, recognizing the Vicar of Christ supreme in matters spiritual, and also because her heart is too much interested in the next world, and not sufficiently devoted to this one; third, the Church looks upon herself as a sort of king in the sense that she claims to be the unique Church of Christ, and refuses absolutely to accept the democratic principle that one religion is just as good as another. Such are, I believe, the three principal complaints and charges against the Church today, and to those who urge them I would remind that they are exactly the same charges that were directed against our blessed Lord Himself in His trial before Pilate.

Since the year 26, Pontius Pilate had been procurator in the name of Tiberius Caesar. Little was known of him before that time. He had been in Judea only a few years, but long enough to draw upon himself the bitterest hate of those over whom he ruled. Sometime before the trial, Pilate had come from Caesarea to Jerusalem to take up winter quarters, bringing with him not only effigies of Caesar on the army banners, but even images of Roman eagles, which he introduced in the temple, without the knowledge of the Jewish people, when the city was asleep. They asked Pilate to remove them, but he would not for fear of injuring Caesar. For five days and nights they stormed about him, and on the sixth day he erected a judgment seat in the open city behind which he concealed his soldiers. The moment they repeated their request Pilate told them they would all be killed if they did not leave off disturbing him. But they threw themselves on the ground and laid their necks bare and said they would rather taste death than transgress the wisdom of their fathers. Pilate, deeply affected, ordered the images removed.

The Jews hated Pilate. They did not forget this incident, nor the time when he introduced votive tablets to the Emperor in Herod's palace in Jerusalem, nor when he confiscated the money of the temple to provide luxurious baths such as he had in Rome, and put down a revolt against his authority with naked swords and enjoyed his ablutions and Jewish money in comparative peace.

That Friday, at dawn, Pontius Pilate, wrapped in toga, still sleepy and yawning, was waiting for a mob in Herod's palace, very ill-disposed towards the trouble-makers who forced him to rise at such an early hour. The crowd of accusers and the rough populace finally came to the front of his palace, but they stopped outside. Why? Because before Pilate's judgment seat, on the paved stones of the Lithostratos, was painted a long white line, marking the boundaries beyond which no Jew could pass without becoming defiled. If they entered the house of a pagan, they were contaminated, and could not eat the Passover. So Caiphas, Annas, and the other accusers stopped at the line.

The hypocrites! They were not afraid of innocent blood, but they were afraid of a white line.

Pilate went to that line and asked abruptly: "What accusation bring you against this man?" The Jews knew very well they could not win Pilate's favor if they charged the Christ with attacks upon the religion of their fathers. They were, therefore, ready to lie. Those who are bent upon evil look upon an accessory infamy as of little consequence. Pilate, they knew, could be conquered only by appealing to his loyalty to Rome and to the Emperor. They would give a political coloring to the accusation. If they told him what they told Annas and Caiphas, that Christ was a false Messiah, Pilate would smile, yea, sneer; but if they said He was a seditious inciter of revolt, that He was stirring up the people against the government, that He was unpatriotic, that He was inimical to the best interests of their country, Pilate could do no less than put Him to death. In other words, the charge of blasphemy is abandoned as soon as they enter the praetorium, and the charge of sedition is taken up. The judgment against our Lord shifts now from religious grounds, where it had been laid before Annas and Caiphas, to patriotic grounds before Pilate. Note the irony of it all!

These same people who had risen against Pilate's authority, who hated him as a Roman, as a symbol of foreign domination and their own slavery, who hated him still more as Pontius Pilate, as plotter against their religion, and thief of their money—these very people now drown their hate, protest their loyalty to Caesar, their affection for his security, their readiness to accept no Caesar but him because they had found a new hate, a new enemy—Christ Jesus our Lord.

And up against the marble balustrade of Pilate's judgment seat, the charges rolled, and they were three:

FULTON J. SHEEN

We have found this man perverting our nation.
He has forbidden us to give tribute to Caesar.
He says He is Christ, the King. (Luke 23:2)

The same charges brought against the Church today! Every word was a lie! He was not perverting the nation; He was bringing balm to wounded hearts and healing to palsied limbs; He was making of that unhappy and degraded people a blessed kingdom of saints. "I am come that you may have life, and may have it more abundantly." "Come to me, all you that labor, and are burdened, and I will refresh you." He was not refusing to give tribute to Caesar. Had not the Scribes and the Pharisees already been convinced this was not true when they asked: "Is it lawful to give tribute to Caesar?" and heard in answer the divine reply: "Render to Caesar the things that are Caesar's, and to God, the things that are God's." He was not attempting to make Himself King, for one day when the people would have taken Him by force and made Him King, He fled away into the mountain alone.

In this trial before Pilate there is unfolded the whole history of the Church in relation to the world. The charges brought against our Lord—all false—are the same charges brought against the Church today. And what is particularly striking about them all is that patriotism is made the cloak for them all. There is nothing so sublime that cannot be prostituted, and even the noble virtue of patriotism may have its prostitutors. Old Samuel Johnson once truly said that "patriotism is the last refuge of a *scoundrel*," and how true, for just as many sins are committed in its name as in the name of liberty.

As the accusers of our blessed Lord covered themselves with the assumed virtue of patriotism, so do the enemies of the Church, and their charges are just as untrue and unwarranted as the charges directed against our blessed Lord Himself. First, the Church is not perverting the nation. If our nation has any ideal at all, it certainly has the ideal of *stability*, which means that it must resolve to survive and to march steadily onward in the vanguard of civilization. Now I ask you, what forces are best suited to give to our government this very desirable *stability*? Will the forces of birth control, which limits the number of our citizens by refusing to bring into the world the very units of democratic social life, make for its stability? Will the loose divorce laws of our country, which break up families, the very core of national life, make for its endurance? Will the loose morality, which believes that anything is right, providing one is not caught, make for a strong and disciplined and stable nation? These are the forces which are decaying and breaking down our national life. But the only single force in America today which opposes these destructive elements is the spiritual force of the Church. By what logic, then, can the Church be said to be perverting the nation? If in centuries to come there are eyes to look upon the flag and there are lungs to breathe the air of freedom and there are hearts to respond to America's anthem, it will be because there is a divine power operating in American life, teaching that marriage is a sacred thing and that the children of today are the citizens of tomorrow. Break up husband and wife, and you break the family; break the family, you break the children; break them, and you wreck a nation. That is just what the Church is trying to avert, and in doing so, instead of perverting the nation, the Church is making it stable enough to endure, that in centuries to come it may draw down upon itself the blessings of a pleased and Almighty Father.

Second, the Church is not refusing to give full tribute to America, and because her spiritual head is in Rome it no more follows that he loves his country less than does any citizen of this land whose mother is in the green isle of Ireland. The Church and the State belong to two distinct spheres, and there may be, therefore, a true and loyal allegiance to both, for we are to "render to Caesar the things that are Caesar's, and to God the things that are God's." As a matter of fact, only those who love the spiritual can ever love the natural. Full and loving service of the Church of Christ no more conflicts with the love of nation than the love of the soul is at variance with the love of the body. The loves, paradoxical though they may seem, merge into unity, thanks to the charity of our Sovereign Head who loved his own country even to the point of weeping over its capital city, and shedding the salt tears of the first Christian patriot. He who reserved the first fruits of His message for the lost sheep of Israel was the same One whose flame of charity embraced the whole world, and whose life was surrendered on the gibbet of a cross for the redemption of all peoples, for all climes and all times.

St. Francis of Assisi loved his own country to the passionate degree that on dying, he asked to be carried to a hill to see and bless for the last time his beloved countryside; and yet, that love of nationalism no way prevented that soul of his from embracing not only man, but the beasts and birds, not only the fires and the forests, but above all, the spiritual father of Christendom, who gave him the right to found an order which today lights the torches of its charity at the fiery heart of that same poor man of Assisi. St. Paul, too, loved his own country, was proud of being of the race of Abraham, a Hebrew and a son of a Hebrew, but the love for his own people in no way conflicted with those wider interests where there are no distinctions between Jew and Greek, barbarian and freeman, but only the consuming love to be dissolved and to be with Christ.

THE CHRIST

And what is true of Francis and Paul is true of each loyal son of the Church. We Catholics will give way to no one in the depth of our allegiance to America, and in our allegiance to America we will give way to no one in our allegiance to Christ. Finally, it is not true that the Church is calling herself a King, and is flying in the face of the democratic principle of equality. What is the foundation of equality? Do those doctrines which hold that one-fifth of the population of this country, the Catholic population, is unpatriotic, make for true patriotism of equality? Will the jingoism of the superiority of the Nordic over the Latin make for true equality? Will the mere lip-worship of the brotherhood of man or the singing of a common anthem reduce men to unity? The fact is men do not naturally love men. Beauty is a stronger attraction than the mere cry of equality and fraternity. Where find, then, the real force behind equality? There is only one foundation for equality, and that is the Catholic doctrine that all men have been redeemed by the precious blood of Jesus Christ, that all men have been called to share His life, and that President and citizen, poor and rich, the mighty and the lowly, have been thought so much worth while that Christ would have died for the least of them; that the beggar in the Bowery and the man in the gilded apartment are equal in the eyes of God. And in order to impress this unity on her people, the Church preaches the doctrine of the Eucharist, in which every communicant partakes of the same bread in order that they might have the same life, for eating the one Bread, they are the one Body. The Church thus gives to humanity a new beauty and a new reason for loving all men. There is no power in the world making for equality amongst men, so capable of drawing them together into holy bonds of peace and love, so destined to melt all differences of race and blood as the communion-rail of the Catholic

Church for there equality is based upon common purity of heart in Christ Jesus our Lord.

The three charges have found popular expression in words uttered not so long ago by the so called philosopher, Bertrand Russell, who said that a grave danger faces America, for in one hundred and fifty years it will be Catholic. I am not so sure that in one hundred and fifty years America will be Catholic, but if it is to be Catholic, it will have to do two more things than it is doing now: it will have to begin to think, and it will have to begin to pray.

Just suppose that that prophecy of Bertrand Russell's did come true. Suppose that everyone in America were Catholic. Suppose that every citizen tomorrow morning knelt down and said his prayers to God. Suppose that as each citizen went to work—the doctor to his patient, the judge to his bench, the lawyer to his court, the clerk to his office, the employee to his employer—each and every one of them was convinced that someday they would have to render an account for even the least actions of their daily life, although unseen by men. Suppose that all the children went to a school where they heard the name of God, and drank in sweet stories about His Mother and the saints. Suppose that the students who went to universities learned not vague theories about sex, but the beauty of chastity, bringing the reward of the vision of God. Suppose that all the divorce courts of our land closed, and that about once every month every man, woman and child would kneel at the communion-rail and receive into his very soul the very God who died on the cross for them. Do you think that would be a menace to American life? If that is a menace, then peace is a menace, then justice is a menace, then charity is a menace, then Christ is a curse!

May all such un-Christian sentiments and every inhuman sentiment pass from our midst, and as days roll into weeks, and weeks into years, may one lesson more and more become deeply embedded in the consciousness of our national life, and that lesson is the message of this discourse: that Catholics will never love America because she is great, but America will be great because Catholics love her.

THE CHURCH AND THE TIMES

DELIVERED ON MARCH 6, 1932

ONE of the catchwords which keeps unthinking minds from Truth and Life is the phrase: "The Church is behind the times." The "acids of modernity" are supposed to have eaten away traditional morality, and yet the Church clings on to the same beliefs and practices held centuries ago. Not only that, but if we are to believe her critics, the Church never does the worldly thing. The worldly thing to do today, according to the modern mind, is to accept divorce and birth control as progressive and forward-looking practices, and yet the Church refuses to compromise, even in the slightest, her centuries-old teaching, that she might harmonize the better with the demands of the twentieth century.

Thousands of people, it is said, would join the Church tomorrow if she would only relax her moral discipline, or re-adjust her idea of God to suit the new astrophysics, or recognize divorce as the Christian sects have done. But the Church remains adamant: the world asks for one thing, the Church gives it another. "If she will not change, then she shall die," is the pronouncement of modern prophets.

As modern as this charge is, let us turn back the scroll of history to see just how ancient it is, and we shall discover that Herod condemned our blessed Lord on exactly the same ground that the world today condemns the Church.

Herod was that type which might be characterized as a splendid animal. Descended as he was from Herod the Great, who murdered his own wife and slaughtered the children of Bethlehem, the younger Herod combined gross sensuality with an artistic temperament, which manifested itself in his fine taste for buildings. These he was always careful to dedicate to the Emperor. As governor of Galilee, living at Tiberias on the shore of the sea, he often came up to Jerusalem for the great feasts of the Jews, stopping at the house of his half-brother, Phillip. There he seduced his brother's wife, Herodias, and her young daughter, Salome, and drove his own wife, daughter of Aretas, King of Arabia, from his own house.

Sinful life always palls, after its brief hour, and Herod was obliged to seek new thrills for his already jaded life. News came to him that down along the banks of the Jordan, amid the tamarisks and green trees lining its banks, there was a strange and eloquent man who lived on wild locusts, who was clothed in camel's skin, and whose name was John the Baptist.

Not because he was interested in John's doctrine, but because, as for so many in our day, religion was interesting only as an emotional outlet, Herod summoned the saint, and bade him come unto him. John accepted. The court was delighted. They were eager to hear his rugged eloquence, and just for a moment to feel their wearied and wasted systems awakened to new life by the strange and novel sensation of a sermon in the house of Gold.

At the appointed hour, the man whom our Lord had called "the greatest man of woman born" stepped into the temporary pulpit erected for him in the courtroom. From the worldly point of view, the proper thing for John to have done on such an occasion, would have been to flatter the vices and the excesses of the king. The unworldly and impolitic thing would have been to condemn the adulterous life of Herod. John, keen on pleasing

God rather than man, stretched out his hand to the throne, pointed directly to the one sitting there, and thundered: "It is not lawful for thee to have thy brother's wife." That was not the worldly thing to do. Before he was aware, chains were about his wrists and iron bars before his eyes. How differently many a modern preacher would have acted!

The birthday of Herodias soon approached, and lest silence should throw Herod back on his conscience and perhaps on salvation, he planned a mighty banquet. Everything that could satisfy a tongue was served. Bronzed slaves ministered to the appetite with all the delicacies of the fishery, the fields and the vineyards. The tetrarch Herod became full of wine. He gave a signal and great purple curtains at the end of the banquet hall parted, disclosed the sparingly clad form of Salome, daughter of Herodias and Phillip, her lawful husband. Accompanied by slow, voluptuous music, the girl danced with the wild abandon of her passionate theme. Herod, his eyes sealed upon her, became maddened more with the dance than with the wine. Before the curtain had time to drop, the tetrarch, giddy with extreme pleasure, sent for the girl, bidding her tell him what love-token she would have, swearing to her that if it be half his kingdom, it should be hers. The child, well-schooled by her mother, answered: "Give me here in a dish the head of John the Baptist."

Before the music had completely ceased, a guardsman was seen crossing the threshold, bearing aloft on a silver charger the head of John.

The vision of that decapitated head haunted Herod. One day he heard talk of the miracles of our blessed Lord, and he remarked to one of his courtiers: "This is John the Baptist; he has risen from the dead." From that time on, he kept close watch over our Lord. One day a Pharisee came to our Lord and said to

Him: "Depart, and get thee hence, for Herod hath a mind to kill thee." Our Lord answered by calling Herod a "fox." Weeks and months passed, and in Jerusalem, before the murderer of John and the son of the murderer of the babes of Bethlehem, stood the One whom John had announced, the grown Babe of Bethlehem, now the Man of Nazareth. And Herod was glad. Glad at such a moment? Yes! St. Luke, describing the scene, tells us that he was "very glad" for he hoped to see some miracle done by Him.

Herod greeted our Lord as he would have accosted a performer who might enter his court to while away the tedium of an hour. He received the Son of God as a sensational wonder-man, who might amuse a jaded, profligate court by a startling trick of magic, or a marvel of jugglery. He wanted the sensational and the new to gratify his curiosity. It was his nerves, not his soul, that wanted a thrill. After all, according to Herod, was not the world given for enjoyment of every fleeting moment, was not the human being born into the world to have a good time, to rob monotony of its victory?

Herod questioned our Lord, and we can well imagine what his questions were: "How did you escape the massacre instituted by my father at Bethlehem? And why did you call me a fox? And what was the meaning of your triumphal entry into Jerusalem last Sunday?"

To all the questions our Lord gave only the answer of His withering silence. He who spoke to sinful Magdalene, to the woman taken in adultery, to little children, to deceitful Annas, to mean Caiphas, to weak Pilate, now refused to utter a single word to the one man who could save Him from crucifixion.

From a worldly point of view, our Lord did the foolish thing, just as John before Him did the foolish thing. What would you think of a man in court who might clear himself of the charges against him by a word, a show of power, and yet who refused to do so? Here is our Lord going to the cross and to death, simply because He will not do the worldly thing. Herod wanted one thing; Christ gave him another. Herod wanted a trick, something to relieve the intolerable monotony of his sensuous life. He wanted fireworks, and He who claimed to be the Light of the World offered him light instead, the white flame without flicker of a divine Personality in the lantern of His sacred Humanity. That was foolishness! The folly of Omnipotence! And so Herod robed Him in the garment of a fool!

And from that day to this, the Church has been robed in the garment of a fool because she never does the worldly thing. Her saints are fools because they plunge after poverty while other men dig after gold; her saints crucify their bodies, as other men pamper them, they dare "to swing the earth a trinket at their wrist," while others prostrate themselves before it. Her devout nuns are fools who leave the lights and glamours of the world for the shades and shadows of the cross, where saints are made. Her priests are fools, because they practice celibacy in a world which has gone mad about sex. The Vicar and Pontiff is a fool for refusing to relax the doctrine of Christ concerning the sanctity of marriage, when every Christian sect under the sun has relaxed it. Yes, the Church is a fool, and all her faithful members are fools, but they are fools only from the world's point of view, not from God's point of view. For with the foolish things of the world hath God chosen to confound the wise, and with the weak things of the world, to confound the strong.

The Church must always bear the taunt of being unmodern and unworldly, as our Lord had to bear it before Herod. And the divine Master warned us that it would be the mark of the divinity of the Church. "I have taken you out of the world…therefore the world will hate you... If I had left you in the world, the world would love its own... Remember, it hath hated me before you." In other words, if you ever want to discover divine religion on the face of the earth, look for the Church that does not get along with the world. The religion that gets on with the world and is accepted by the world is worldly; the religion that does not get on with the world is other-worldly, which is another way of saying that it is divine.

But because the Church is other-worldly, and seeks first the Kingdom of God and His justice, it must not be thought that it is out of touch with the world. The Church is not behind the times; it is beyond the times. It is not modern; it is ultra-modern. It is not a slave to the fashions of the twentieth century, for it must keep its head to serve the thirtieth century. The Church is very modern if modern means serving the times in which we live, but it is not modern if it means believing that whatever is modern is true. The Church is modern if modern means that her members should change their hats with the seasons, and even with the styles, but it is not modern if it means that every time a man changes his hat, he should also change his head, or in an applied sense, that the Church should change its idea of God every time psychology puts on a new shirt, or physics a new coat.

It is modern if modern means incorporating the new-found wisdom of the present into the patrimony of the centuries, but it is not modern if it means sneering at the past as one might sneer at a lady's age. It is modern if modern means a passionate desire to know the truth, but it is not modern if it means that truth changes with the calendar, and that what is true on Friday is false on Saturday. The Church is modern if modern means progress toward a fixed ideal, but she is not modern if it means changing the ideal instead of attaining it.

FULTON J. SHEEN

The Church is like an old schoolmaster, the schoolmaster of the centuries, and as such it has seen so many students pass before it, cultivate the same poses and fall into the same errors, that it merely smiles at those who believe that they have discovered a new truth, for in the Church's superior wisdom and experience, it knows that many a so-called new truth is but the new label for an old error. Experience has taught it that the modernism of 1932 is not the modernism of 1942, and that what one generation believes to be true, the next will believe to be false; and that the surest way to be a widow in the next age is to marry the spirit of this one. Today the Church is accused of being behind the times, because it does not go mad about Freud. I dare say that in fifty years from now if one of the teachers in any of our great universities mounted his rostrum and talked Freud, he would be considered just as antiquated and behind the times as a politician who today might mount a soap-box at the corner of Forty-second and Broadway, and open a campaign for William McKinley as President.

It is about time that the modern world gave up expecting the Church to die, because she is "behind the times." Really, she is behind the scenes, and knows just when the curtain will fall on each new fad and fancy. If an announcement had been made a thousand times about a death, and the funeral never took place, men would soon begin to take the funeral as a joke. And so it is with the Church. She is always supposed to be behind the times, and yet it is she who lives beyond the times. At least a hundred men in every century since her birth, have tolled the bells for her funeral, but the corpse has never appeared. They are always buying coffins for her, and use the coffins themselves. They are always assisting at her apparently last breath, and yet she moves amid their dust. They are always digging her grave, and it is a grave into which the diggers fall. The taunt that she is behind the times and out of touch with the world will never bother her, for she knows that it is easy to be in the swim, in the sense of being up to the times, for even a dead body can float downstream. It takes a live body to resist the current. It is easy to say we should change our morality to suit the so-called new ideas about sex, just as it was easy to say a few centuries ago that one should be a Calvinist. It is always easy to let the world have its way; the difficult thing and the noble thing is to keep God's way. It is easy to fall; there are a thousand angles at which a thing will fall, but there is only one at which it will stand, and that is the angle at which the Church is poised between heaven and earth, and from the angle she has sung a requiem over all the prophets of the past who ever said she was dying, and she will continue to chant requiems over all the prophets of the future, for the story of her life is the story of John in the courtroom of Herod.

Salome danced, and as she danced she kept pace with the time, to be the earthly symbol of all those who change to keep up with the times. As she danced, two men lost their heads, Herod lost his head figuratively, for he believed that a man should change with the times, and that it was lawful to live with another man's wife. John lost his head literally, for he believed that a man should not change with the times, and that it was not lawful to live with the wife of another. The Church believes that John was right, and Herod wrong, and being a saint, which is the foolishness which purchases eternity, means losing one's head John's way rather than Herod's.

THE CRUCIFIXION

DELIVERED ON MARCH 13, 1932

FOUR judges sat in judgment against the Lord and Savior of the world, and they condemned Him to death on contradictory charges. He was accused of being too dogmatic before Caiphas, because He enunciated the doctrine of His divinity; He was accused of being too undogmatic before Annas, because He refused to make any additional pronouncements concerning His doctrine and His ministry; He was accused of being too worldly before Pilate, because He was perverting the nation; He was accused of being too unworldly before Herod, because He refused to do the worldly thing, and perform a trick of magic to gain His release. Too dogmatic, too undogmatic! Too worldly, too unworldly! Men could not agree on why He should die, but they did agree that He should die. Where find a fitting punishment for one condemned on contradictory charges? The only fitting death for one condemned on contradictory charges is not scourging, nor stoning, but the crucifixion, for on the cross one bar is at variance or contradiction with another.

And so the King went to His death—for a bed, a cross; for a pillow, a crown of thorns; and lest His hands and feet should slip out, they tucked them in with nails. A King is hanging from a peg—aye, more than a King—Truth, Justice, Mercy, God.

And the three great civilizations of the world saw Him hang, and suffer, and die, for He was crucified in the language of Hebrew, Latin and Greek, in the civilizations of Jerusalem, Rome and Athens, in the name of religion, law and morality, in the name of the good, the true and the beautiful. Jerusalem was the city of religion, and it condemned the One who brought it religion; Latin Rome was the city of law, and it condemned the Lawmaker; Athens was the city of morality, and it condemned the Sinless. Representatives of each of these civilizations passed beneath the banner of the cross, and hurled the challenge each in their own language: "Come down from the cross and we will believe." What happened in those terrible moments of hate was not something that would pass into history, like the battle of Marathon; what was happening was the first scene in an abiding drama, the curtain of which will not ring down until the crack of doom. It is now the Mystic Christ, or the Church, which is hanging on the cross, and today just as twenty centuries ago, she is being crucified in the modern civilization of Jerusalem, Rome, and Athens, in the name of modern religion, modern law, and modern morality.

Modern irreligion marches beneath the cross, looks up to the Church crucified thereon by an unbelieving world, and who is there who has not heard it say at least a thousand times: "Come down from your belief in infallibility. Come down from your belief in the primacy of Peter. Come down from your attachment to the divinity of Christ. Come down from your devotion to the Virgin Mary and the Saints. Come down from your belief that you are the one, true, unique spouse, the Church of Christ. Can you not see that there are other crosses on Calvary besides your own? Come down and we will believe!"

And next, modern law, modern in the sense that it has broken with Christian tradition, takes its stand beneath the cross, and who is there who is not already familiar with its taunts and pleadings: "Come down from your belief in the law of eternal justice. Come down from your belief in hell. Come down from your belief that the laws of Christ are more sound than the laws of the State. Come down from your belief in the law of mortification, for who is there in the pagan world who wants your penance and your suffering? Look to the sorry end it has brought you now. Come down from your cross, and we will believe!"

And finally, the third of the enduring civilizations, the teachers of modern morality, advances beneath the same cross, and who is there living in this great era of carnality who has not heard its taunts a thousand times as it sneers at the Church: "Come down from your belief in the sanctity of marriage. Come down from your belief in virginity and celibacy. Come down from your age-long opposition to divorce. Come down from your opposition to sex, when all the world is agog with sex. Come down from your opposition to birth control. Can you not see that the acids of modernity have eaten away your age-old morality? Come down from the cross, and we will believe!"

But the Church does not come down, though ten thousand times ten thousand tongues are loud in their pleading, and it does not come down, because Christ did not come down. It is easy to step down from great heights when the world scorns, but it is the sign of a martyr to die for an ideal. It is easy to come down and follow the world, but it is nobler to remain suspended and draw the world to oneself. It is human to come down, but it is divine to hang there.

But will there never be a reconciliation between the world and the Church? Must the one always be hanging on the cross in apparent defeat, and the other walking the earth in apparent victory? Ah, there is the possibility of a reconciliation, and it resides in the words of forgiveness pronounced the first time by our blessed Lord on the cross, and now repeated for the thousandth time by the Church on its cross.

And what were those words? They were words of a prayer—words that fell in a voice calm and low, heard above the shaking of dice, the moans of dying thieves, the sobs of a Magdalene, and the sighs of a Mary—a prayer heard in heaven and earth—a prayer that went out from Calvary's hills and reechoes to our own ears today: "Father, forgive them, for they know not what they do."

Forgive whom? Forgive those who crucify in the name of modern religion, modern law and modern morality, in the language of Hebrew and Latin and Greek? Forgive them? Why? Because they know what they do? No, because they know not what they do! It is only the ignorance of what is involved in their great crime which brings them within the pale of the mercy of the One on the cross, and the forgiveness of the heavenly Father. It is solely and uniquely because they know not what they do that there is a possibility of forgiveness. There is not redemption for the fallen angels, simply because they knew what they were doing. But we do not always know what we are doing. If we did, and still did it, we would never be saved. It is not wisdom that saves! It is ignorance!

Will Annas be forgiven because he knew the Talmud from beginning to end? Will Caiphas be forgiven because he knew the details of the law of the Sanhedrin? Will Pilate be forgiven because he knew Roman law? Will Herod be forgiven because he knew how to be a tetrarch? Will the followers of modern religion, modern law and modern morality, be forgiven because of what they know? They know something about Einstein's theory and the necessity of a cosmical religion; they know the latest book of the month, and the new morals which have supplanted Christianity; they know all the spurious arguments in favor of birth control; they know the new psychological theory emanating from Vienna in which the soul is reduced to sex; they know the movement of world politics; they know the world, its ways, its sin, its crime, its fiction—they know all these things and they are proud of what they know, and yet not a single one of them will be saved because of what he knows. They will come within the fold of divine forgiveness only on condition that they learn to know that they do not know everything. If their learning is going to make them proud of rejecting Christ and the moral laws; if it is going to make them dispense with redemption as a pagan myth, conscience as an illusion, God as an idea—then they will never be happy, then they will never be saved. Why, they would be damned if it were not for their ignorance of the terrible thing they are doing when they leave God and Christ out of their lives. It is not wisdom that saves—it is ignorance!

Will the executioners be saved because they knew what they did when they unfurled our blessed Lord like a wounded eagle upon the banner of salvation? Will the bigots who say all manner of evil things against the Church, her priests, her doctrine, her faithful; will the leaders of Bolshevism who attempt to root out religion from the hearts of people as if it were an opiate; will those who spread venomous lies about the Vicar of Christ, our gloriously reigning Pius XI—will all those whose love for modern religion, modern law and modern morality, which can find no other expression or outlet except in cries of hate and bitterness—will all those who persecute the Church and thus nail Christ anew to the cross be saved because they know what they are doing? It is only because they are ignorant of what the Church really is, that they are brought within hearing of the cry of the cross. If Saul knew what he was doing in persecuting the Church of Damascus, when Christ called out to him from the heavens, he would never have become Paul. So, too, if modern

Sauls knew what they were doing in persecuting the Church, and knowing what they did, even with the heavens rent and Christ telling them they were persecuting Him, they would be cast into hell. It is not wisdom that saves—it is ignorance!

Every true follower of Christ knows he must be hated by the world. "I have taken you out of the world," said our blessed Lord, "therefore, the world will hate you. If I had left you in the world, the world would have loved you. Remember it hath hated me before you; the servant is not above his Master." We must be hated even as Christ Himself was hated. We must be abused as Christ Himself was abused. We must be prepared to be told a thousand times over that we are ignorant because we do not know that modern psychology has disproven a soul; that we are benighted fools because we do not know that higher Biblical criticism has destroyed the authenticity of Scripture; that we are narrow-minded because we do not accept the unmoral inter-pretations of God's laws; that we are a race of darkened minds because we do not know that evolution has proven original sin to be a myth; that we are ignorant because we do not know that science has dispensed with Providence, with God, and with Christ.

Yes, we are ignorant! Ignorant of the false wisdom of the world; ignorant of the wisdom of the age; ignorant of all that false wisdom which would blind us to the lightening truths of the Eternal Sun; ignorant of modern pagan ways. Oh, Holy Father in Heaven, we thank thee we are ignorant—ignorant of those things which keep us from thee! It is not the wisdom of the world that saves—it is ignorance!

Hence, there is not a loyal Catholic heart in the world, kneel-ing at the foot of the cross, that is ignorant of the reason of all forgiveness, and from such a heart comes the plaintive prayer:

FULTON J. SHEEN

"Oh, Jesus, I do not want to know the world; I do not want to know the pride of the world which crowns thy head with thorns; I do not want to know how nails of selfishness are driven, nor how the spear of bitterness is launched; I do not want to know how snowflakes are hammered, nor who turns about the Arcturus; I do not want to know the length of this great universe and its expanse in light years; I do not want to know the breadth of the earth as it dances about the chariot of the sun; I do not want to know the heights of the stars as they glitter about the day's dead sanctities; I do not want to know the depth of the sea, nor the secrets of its palace. I am willing to be ignorant of all these things. I want to know only one thing, and that is—the breadth and length and depth and height of thy redeeming love on the cross, sweet Savior of men. I want, dear Jesus, to be ignorant of everything in this world—everything—but you! And then, by the strangest of strange paradoxes, I shall be wise."

THE ETERNITY OF EASTER

DELIVERED ON MARCH 27, 1932

MY Easter wish is that your soul may be flooded with the peace and joy which comes from the victory of the Risen Christ, who bears now and forevermore not wounds, but scars as pledges of love and forgiveness.

The birth of our Savior was announced to a Virgin, but in order that we poor sinners might have hope, the Resurrection was first announced to a sinner. On the first Easter morning, Mary Magdalen went to the sepulchre expecting to find her Master there. All things else might have been a failure, but at least in His grave could be followed the object of her love. Nothing else might have been left for her: the voice, the manners, the living presence, the strong tender words, the works of charity—all these she thought were passed. But there was one thing left and that was the mangled form lying in a grave. This she would honor and as once before she broke the alabaster box and poured out ointment on His feet, so now she would break her heart and pour it out in tears upon His grave. She was not looking forward, but only to the past. In the words of St. John: early in the morning when it was yet dark, she came unto the sepulchre and stood weeping, and as she looked into the sepulchre she saw two Angels in white, sitting one at the head and one at the foot where the body of Christ had been laid. They sayeth to her: "Woman, why weepest thou?" She sayeth to them: "Because they have taken away my Lord and I know not where they have laid Him."

When she had thus spoken she turned herself back, and saw Jesus standing, and she knew not that it was Jesus.

Jesus said to her: "Woman, why weepest thou? Whom seekest thou?" She, thinking it was the gardener, sayeth to Him: "Sir, if thou hast taken Him hence, tell me where thou hast laid Him, and I will take Him away." And Jesus said to her: "Mary." She turning, sayeth to Him: "Rabboni." And as she cast herself at His feet, she saw the two livid marks of nails. But before they could be embraced, Jesus said to her: "Do not touch me for I am not yet ascended to my Father. But go to my brethren, and say to them: I ascend to my Father and to your Father, to my God and to your God."

To Mary, the supreme object of faith could be touched by fingers; she could only think of Rabboni whose feet could be clasped; her soul was dominated by time; she was content with an unfinished work; and the words of our blessed Savior to her revealed the truth that He was no longer to be seen under the form of time and in the world of sensations, but only by the soul and in the world of eternity. So the first lesson of Easter morn, the lesson that Mary failed to comprehend, in the words of St. Paul, was "if you be risen with Christ seek the things that are above where Christ sitteth at the right hand of God: mind the things that are above, not the things that are upon the earth."

This great truth needs to be stressed strongly on this new Easter Day when men no longer speak of eternity, but only of time; when they are more concerned about citizenship in the Kingdom of this world than citizenship in the Kingdom of Heaven; when their interests center more around passing questions of science, politics, economics, wealth and power, instead of around the Risen Christ who sitteth eternally at the right hand of God. Some of our modern minds have so departed from the

Gospel of the Resurrection and its emphasis on eternity as to make the time element of physics the very fabric of the universe. Sacred Scripture tells us that a moment will come when there will be no more time. The unsacred scripture of our day tells us that time is the very essence of things.

In order that we might know that the real peace and happiness is not in time but in eternity with the Risen Christ and the glory of His Father and the love of His Holy Spirit, I propose to show first of all, that time stands in the way of real happiness, and second, that only inasmuch as we succeed in rising above time in this world, do we ever begin to be happy.

Time is the one thing that makes real pleasure impossible. By its very nature it forbids us to have many pleasures together under the penalty of having none of them at all. By the mere fact that I exist in time, it is impossible for me to combine the pleasures of marching with the Old Guard of Napoleon, and at the same time advancing under the Flying Eagles of Caesar. By the mere fact that I live in time, I cannot enjoy simultaneously the winter sports of the Alps and the limpid waters of the Riviera. Time makes it impossible for me to be stirred by the oratory of a Demosthenes, and at the same time to listen to the melodious accents of the great Bossuet. Time does not permit me to combine the prudence that comes with age, and the buoyancy that belongs to youth. It is the one thing which prevents me from gathering around the same festive table with Aristotle, Socrates, and Thomas Aquinas in order to learn the secrets of the great minds in solving the riddles of a universe. If it were not for time, Dante and Shakespeare could have sipped tea together, and Homer even now might tell us his stories in English. It is all very nice and lovely to enjoy the mechanical perfections of this age of luxury, but there are moments when I would like to enjoy the calm and peace of the Middle Ages, but time will not permit it. If I live in the twentieth century, I must sacrifice the pleasures of the thirteenth century, and if I enjoy the Athenian Age of Pericles, I must be denied the Florentine Age of Dante.

All things are good, and yet none can be enjoyed except in their season, and the enjoyment must always be tinged with the regret that time will demand their surrender. Time gives me things, but it also takes them away. When it does give, it gives but singly, and thus life becomes but just one fool thing after another.

This thought suggests the suspicion that if time makes the combination of pleasures impossible, then if I could ever transcend time, I might in some way increase my happiness, and this I find to be true, for every conscious desire to prolong a pleasure is a desire to make it an enduring "now." Like cats before the fire, we want to prolong the pleasure indefinitely; we want it to be permanent and not successive.

Go back in the storehouse of your memory, and you will find ample proof that it is always in those moments when you are least conscious of the passing of time that you most thoroughly enjoy yourself. How often it happens, for example, when listening to an absorbing conversation or the thrilling experiences of a much-travelled man, that the hours pass by so quickly we are hardly conscious of them. We say, "The time passes like everything." What is true of a delightful conversation is also true of aesthetic pleasures. I dare say that very few would ever notice the passing of time while listening to an orchestra translate the beauty of one of Beethoven's overtures. In just the proportion that it pleases and thrills, it makes us unconscious of how long we were absorbed by its melodies. The contrary fact illustrates the same truth. The more we notice time, the less we are being interested. If our friends keep looking at their watches while we tell a story, we can be very sure that they are being bored by the story. A man who keeps his eye on the clock is not the man who is interested in his work. The more we notice the passing of time, the less is our pleasure, and the less we notice the passing of time, the greater is our pleasure.

These psychological facts of experience testify that not only is time the obstacle of enjoyment, but escape from it is the essential of happiness. Suppose we could enlarge upon our experience in such a way as to imagine ourselves completely outside of time and succession, in a world where there would never be a "before" nor an "after" but only a "now."

Suppose we could go out to another existence, where the great pleasures of history would not be denied us because of their historical incompatibility, but all would be unified in a beautiful hierarchical order, like a pyramid in that all would minister to the very unity of our personality. Suppose I say that I could reach a point of timelessness where all the enjoyments and beauties and happiness of time could be reduced to those three fundamental unities which constitute the perfection of my being, namely, life and truth and love, for into these three all pleasures can be resolved.

Suppose first of all, that I could reduce to a single focal point all the pleasures of life, so that in that "now" which never looks before or after, I could enjoy the life that seems to be in the sea when its restless bosom is dimpled with calm, as well as the urge of life that seems to be in all the hill encircling brooks that loiter to the sea; the life which provokes the dumb dead sod to tell its thoughts in violets; the life which pulsates through a spring time blossom as the swinging, cradle for the fruit; the life of the flowers as they open the chalice of their perfume to the sun; the life of the birds as the great heralds of song and messengers of joy; the life of all the children that run shouting to their mothers' arms; the life of all the parents who beget a life like unto their own; the life of the mind that on the wings of invisible thought strikes out to the battlements of eternity, to the life whence all living comes.

Suppose that in addition to concentrating all the life of the universe in a single point, I could also concentrate in another focal point all the truths of the world, so that I could know the truth the astronomer seeks as he looks up through his telescope; and the truth the biologist seeks as he looks down through his microscopes; the truth about the heavens, and who shut up the sea with doors when it did burst forth as issuing out of a womb; the truth about the hiding place of darkness and the treasure house of hail, and the cave of the winds; the truth about the common things; why fire, like a spirit mounts to the heavens heavenly, and why gold, like clay, falls to earth earthly; the truth the philosopher seeks as he tears apart with his mind the very wheels of the universe; the truth the theologian seeks as he uses Revelation to ravel the secrets of God which far surpass those that John heard as he leaned his head upon the breast of the Master.

Suppose that over and above all these pleasures of life and truth, there can be unified in another focal point all the pleasures and beauties of love, that have contributed to the happiness of the universe: the love of the patriot for his country; the love of the soldier for his cause; the love of the scientist for his discovery; the love that seems to be in the flowers as they open their petals to embrace the sun; the love that seems to be in the trees as they outstretch their leafy arms as if to contain the sky; the love of the earth at whose breast all creation drinks the milk of life; the love of mothers, who swing open the great portals of life that a child may see the light of day; the love of friend for friend, to whom one could unpack his heart with his troubles; the love of spouse for spouse; the love of husband and wife; and even the love of angel for angel, and angel for God, with a fire and a heat sufficient to enkindle the hearts of ten thousand times ten thousand worlds.

Suppose that all the pleasures of the world could be brought to these three focal points of life and truth and love, just as the rays of the sun are brought to unity in the sun; and suppose that all the successive pleasures of time could be enjoyed at one and the same "now"; and suppose that these points of unity on which our hearts and minds and souls would be directed, would not merely be three abstractions, but that the focal point in which all the pleasures of life were concentrated would be a life personal enough to be a Father, and that that focal point of Truth in which all the pleasures of truth were concentrated would not merely be an abstract truth, but a Truth personal enough to be a Word or a Son, and that that focal point of love in which all the pleasures of love were concentrated was not merely an abstract love, but a love personal enough to be a Holy Spirit; and suppose that once elevated to that supreme height, happiness would be so freed from limitations that it would include those three as One, not in succession, but with a permanence, not as in time, but as in the timeless—then we would have eternity—then we would have God, then we would have happiness, and that would be heaven.

But will the pleasures of that eternity with the Risen Christ and that enjoyment of Life and Truth and Love which is the Trinity, be in any way comparable to the pleasures of time? Is there anyone on this earth who will tell me about heaven? Certainly, there are three faculties to which one might appeal, namely, to what one has seen, to what one has heard, and to what one can imagine. Will heaven surpass all the pleasures of the eye, and the ear, and the imagination? First of all, will it be as beautiful as some of the things that can be seen? I have seen the Villa d'Este of Rome, with its long lanes of ilox and laurel, and its great avenues of cypress trees, all full of what might be called the vivacity of quiet and living silence; I have seen a sunset on the Mediterranean when two clouds came down like pillars to form a brilliant red tabernacle for the sun, glowing like a golden host; I have seen the towers and the minarets of Constantinople from the harbor pierce through the mist which hung over them like a silken veil; I have seen the chateau country of France and her Gothic cathedrals aspiring heavenwards like prayers; I have seen the beauties of the castles of the Rhine, and the combination of such vision almost made me think of the door-keeper of the Temple of Diana who used to cry out to those who entered: "Take heed to your eye," and so I wonder if the things of eternity will be as beautiful as the combined beauty of all the things which I have seen.

I have not only seen the beauties of nature but I have also heard of others that I have not seen: I have heard of the beauties of the hanging gardens of Babylon, of the pomp and dignity of the palaces of the Doges, of the brilliance and glitter of the Roman Forum as its foundations rocked with the tramp of Rome's resistless legions; I have heard of the splendor of the Temple of Jerusalem as it shone like a jewel of the morning sun; I have heard of the beauties of the garden of paradise, where four-fold rivers flowed through lands rich with gold and onyx, a garden made beautiful as only God knows how to make a beautiful garden; I have heard of countless other beauties and joys of nature which tongue cannot describe, nor touch of brush convey, and I wonder if all the joys and pleasures of heaven will be as great as the combined beauty of all the things of which I have heard.

Beyond what I have heard and seen, there are things which I can imagine: I can imagine a world in which there never would be pain, nor disease, nor death; I can imagine a world wherein every man would live in a castle, and in that commonwealth of castles there would be a due order of justice without complaint or anxiety; I can imagine a world in which the winter would never come, and in which the flowers would never fade, and the sun would never set; I can imagine a world in which there would always be peace, a peace and a quiet without idleness, a profound knowledge of things without research, a constant enjoyment without satiety; I can imagine a world which would eliminate all the evils and diseases and worries of life, and combine all its best joys and happiness, and I wonder if all the happiness of heaven would be like the happiness on earth which I can imagine.

Will eternity be anything like what I have seen, or what I have heard, or what I can imagine? No, eternity will be nothing like anything I have seen, heard or imagined. Listen to the voice of God: "Eye hath not seen, nor ear heard, nor hath it entered into the heart of man to know those things which God hath prepared for those who love Him."

If the timeless so much surpasses time that there can be found no parallel for it, then I begin to understand the great mystery of the shape of the human heart. The human heart is not shaped like a valentine heart, perfect and regular in contour; it is slightly irregular in shape as if a small piece of it were missing out of its side. That missing part may very well symbolize a piece that a spear tore out of the universal heart of humanity on the cross, but it probably symbolizes something more. It may very well mean that when God created each human heart, He kept a small sample of it in heaven, and sent the rest of it into the world of time, where it would each day learn the lesson that it could never be really happy, that it could never be really wholly in love, that it could never be really whole-hearted until it rested with the Risen Christ in an eternal Easter, until it went back again to the timeless to recover the sample which God had kept for it for all eternity.

THE CHRIST

PART TWO

THE FULLNESS OF CHRIST

DEDICATED TO
*Mary, Immaculate Mother of
the Historical Christ and the Mystical Christ,
who didst bring forth the Head of the Church
in Bethlehem and His Mystical Body in Jerusalem,
in token of deep filial love and gratitude.*

INTRODUCTION

THE purpose of the Catholic Hour is to preach Christ and Him Crucified. If therefore any word of mine has been as a lantern shedding light in the dark places of your soul; if any thought of mine has filled the cup of your heart with that Love which the little streams of earthly love could not fill; if any idea has caused the tendrils of affection of one heart to trellis and drape itself about the Sacred Heart; if I have convinced a single soul that there are no scales to weigh the treasures of faith; if I have uncaged a single soul, and freed it for flight into the spiritual atmosphere of divine Love, or made a solitary soul dig where it has fallen, to find the pearl of great price—if in a word, my message borne on the invisible rays of light has drawn one listener to Christ, the Light of the World—then this radio course has been worthwhile, then I have not spoken in vain, then I have not lived in vain.

If there be anyone so illumined, kindly pray for me that I may practice what I preach.

Fulton J. Sheen

LIFE BEGINS AT BIRTH

DELIVERED ON DECEMBER 23, 1931

THERE never has been a greater untruth, and there never will be a greater untruth, than "life begins at forty." That phrase is merely the aged's justification for growing old against their will, a soothing ointment for lost vigor and faded beauty which can never be strong and fresh again. I can understand why a hoary old world should put a premium on age, for the world wants the sympathy of those who grow old with her; but I cannot understand why anyone whose vision is broader than the years and whose hopes are higher than an ivy vine should value age above youth. Anyone with the vaguest understanding either of the world of nature or the world of grace knows that life does not begin at forty. Life begins at birth. There are no other introductions to life than the opening of the womb, either the womb of the great portals of flesh or the womb of the baptismal font—the one begetting us as children of men, the other as children of God.

Religion by its very nature has something to do with birth and therefore with youth. Does not all religious history reveal that the closer we get to God the younger we become, and therefore, the more like children? Thus it may well be that as we grow old in years we grow young in God. But how can we grow younger as we grow older? Answer me this question: What is youthfulness? Youthfulness is proximity to the source of life. A child of four is younger than a child of six because two years closer to the source of life—his parents. A man of twenty is younger than a man of forty because twenty years closer to the source of life—his parents. Now we have another source of life than our parents, namely, God. Hence the closer we get to God the younger we become. And so true is this, that the day on which saints *die*, the Church calls their birthday: *natalitia*. The world celebrates a birthday on the day on which we are born to temporal life; the Church celebrates a birthday on the day on which we are born to eternal life. But in either case: Life begins at birth.

Now look to the other side of the picture. Not only do we become younger and more like children the nearer we get to God, but the closer God gets to us the more He becomes a child. God never came so close to us as in the Incarnation, and then He appeared as a babe.

Why is Christmas the happiest day of the year, if it is not because it is a birthday—not the fortieth, but the first? God might have revealed Himself to us in all the full bloom and blossom of a triumphant King of two score years; He might have canonized maturity by making His life begin at forty—but He actually began it as a child. And to the eternal confusion of those who value age above youth He completed His life work, finished His Father's business, while still in His early thirties. Who then will say that life begins at forty? There is no escape from the tremendous fact of Christmas day, that when God revealed Himself to this poor world of ours, men cried in astonishment: "Why, it is a child." And so it is that the closer we get to God the more we become children, and the closer God gets to us the more He becomes a child.

Is it any wonder then that the Christmas announcement of God's coming to earth, was the announcement of a birth: "*Puer natus est*," "a child is born"? No one in the world ever suspected that the Ancient of the Days who presided at creation would take His throne in that creation as a Babe in a crib, just as no one ever thought He would tell the old men of forty, like Nicodemus, that they must be born again. According to all worldly standards it is the aged who are learned, and yet when Wisdom came to earth He was a child, and when Wise Men came to Wisdom they were told to be like children. Christmas then is the coronation of childhood, the glorification of the young whose hearts are simple, the proclamation to aging hearts that the world need not despair and die, because the Fountain of Youth has come into it with His quickening draughts, to unburden the years, turn time backward, make old things young again—for Christmas is a birthday, the birthday of eternal youth.

If you are still young enough to thrill at the things that never grow old then you will recall the incidents of that day when there rang out over the stillness of an evening breeze, over the white chalk hills of Bethlehem, the peal of angel trumpets announcing: "A child is born." For life begins at birth.

A short time before, you will recall, Mary made a journey from Nazareth to Bethlehem where she was to bring forth in time Him who was begotten in the bosom of the Father from all eternity. As we watch her moving over the sandy path as a vision of purity and light, she was not just a mother bearing an unborn babe; rather was she like a covered ciborium of beautiful flesh bearing within herself the Host who was coming to the world as its Christmas Guest. Nazareth to her was the altar of the Annunciation; she was now leaving it for the communion-rail of Bethlehem in order that the joy of receiving God might be that of the least of the cities of Israel. The very word Bethlehem in Hebrew means "the house of bread," and fittingly did that flesh and blood ciborium bring to this village Him who called Himself the Living Bread descended from Heaven. But Bethlehem's rails had no communicants, as from door to door Mary heard the sad words of those whose hearts are so full of the world that they have no room for the Lord of the world: "There is no room." And so away from the inn of the world's opinions, to the stable of the world's outcasts, that ciborium carried its Host. And as the earth hushed with breathless expectancy, as the stars shone like glittering tapers about the festal earth, as shepherds looked up from their sheep at the sound of the song of their Shepherd, amidst the *Domine non sum dignus* of a woman, and the *Gloria* of celestial choirs, lo—the ciborium is opened! Mary lifts from it the Host and between consecrated fingers holds up the Child before an adoring world with the joyful message of youth and life: "Behold the Lamb of God who takest away the sins of the world."

In the verse of Margie Cannon:

> Around the world she walks tonight,
> Beyond the stark Judean hills,
> Looking for candles men may light
> On their soul's window-sills.

> Now she to Bethlehem is come—
> No tapers burn for Him or her—
> Yet in her heart's ciborium
> To angel's songs she feels Him stir.

> One star is eager for His birth,
> And to the manger at its nod,
> High priestess—she—of heaven and earth,
> Enters to bring forth...God!

THE CHRIST

To those whose life begins at forty this birthday of Christmas *happened* over nineteen hundred years ago; but for those whose life begins at birth it is *happening* now. To the spiritually young there is not just a memory of a cave and a crib, but the abiding vision of a God coming to man. The old say: A Child *was* born. The young say: A Child *is* born. The old use the past tense; the young the present tense. The old see Bethlehem in Israel; the young see Bethlehem in the soul.

Is it not a remarkable thing that the words the angels heard over Bethlehem's hill are identically the same words which the Church sings in her Mass on this Christmas day: "A Child is born"? The Church in her liturgy does not change the tense: it is still in the present. She is young—so young that she never grew old enough to use the past tense. And so on this Christmas day, as if Christmas never happened before, the Church which is so young it can never remember a Christmas that *was*, but only a Christmas that *is*, lifts her voice to announce the glad but startling news: *A Child is born.* There is all the novelty about it for us that there is about any birth. The glittering stars over Bethlehem's hills are now the flickering candles of the altar; the *Gloria in excelsis* of the angels is now the *Gloria* of the men whose hearts are young enough to sing; the stable is the tabernacle; the manger is the ciborium; Bethlehem is the communion-rail. And as we, the shepherds in search of our Shepherd, press to the altar on Christmas morning, we see the re-enactment of the great mystery of the Incarnation. At the communion of the Mass as the priest opens the ciborium of gold, as Mary the high priestess opened the ciborium of her flesh, and between consecrated fingers holds up before our eyes the Host wrapped in the swaddling bands of the white species of bread, lo—the mystery is repeated: a Child is born! "Behold the Lamb of God who takest away the sins of the world." It is wonderful to be so young and fresh as to be able to thrill with the birth of the Babe who never grows old! We who are so young and childlike as to believe that Bethlehem is the House of Bread, and Christmas is the birth of Christ, may seem foolish to those who are old with the sophistication of the world; but in the eyes of God may we not have a vision as children of the spirit, which must always be missed by our elders of the world? We cannot help believing that this very Christmas there is a birth, since He is God. It is all very mysterious just like Bethlehem, but simply because He is God, and we are children, must there not be some things which we cannot understand? In other words there will be mysteries because we are children, and we know nothing; in this we will differ from those who admit no mysteries because they know everything. In our simple faith then on Christmas morn at Mass, we shall say: "Dear God who art a Child, I do not understand how thou, whom the world couldst not contain, can repose in that ciborium of gold; but then neither can I understand how thou couldst repose in the fleshy ciborium of a Mother who is really only thy child, because thou didst make her. I cannot understand how thou canst appear this Christmas in the form of bread to be my food; but then I cannot understand either how on the first Christmas thou couldst appear in the form of a Babe, and laid in a manger, the place of food. I cannot understand how thou canst be born this Christmas on an altar; but then I cannot understand either how thou couldst be born the first Christmas in a stable. None of these mysteries my poor child mind can grasp, but none of them would ever make me doubt thee. There is only one thing that could ever make me doubt Christmas; there is only one thing that could ever make me old enough to doubt thee; and that is, that thou being God shouldst out of love for me be born the first Christmas in a stable, and shouldst refuse on this Christmas out of that same love to be born in the stable of my heart—for what doth it profit thee if thou art born a thousand times in Bethlehem and art not born in the souls of us whom thou didst come to save?"

Christmas then is the solemn day when God becomes a Child, and when we become children, and where we all meet a crib. It is the Birthday of Youth. Children thrill at even the most prosaic things of life, because they can never remember seeing or doing it before. So it is with the Church. She is so young, so fresh, so new-born, that she can never remember a Christmas of yesteryear. That is why she is aglow and tingling with joy at the birth of the Babe. The aging old world is already jaded with its memory, for it believes that life begins at forty. But we who will see Bethlehem again on Christmas morn, and receive the Babe not in our arms but in our hearts, know the world is wrong, for life begins at birth.

That is why the God of a million birthdays chose to win back our hearts by beginning His earthly life as a Babe; that is why old men of forty like Nicodemus must be reborn as children if they are to enter the Kingdom of their God; that is why He, our King, thanked His Father that He had hidden His great truths from the wise and revealed them to the little ones; that is why, if we are ever to return to our true nature, we must get back to where we began as children: "Whosoever shall not receive the Kingdom of God as a little child shall not enter into it." We must get away from our superior wisdom and get back to the faith of a child; we must realize that the possibilities of modern science do not exhaust the possibilities of God; that there is hope for the world not because we grow older and wiser, but because children are born into it who start it all over again. Life begins at birth: that is, we must realize that if we do reach the age of forty we must by the spiritual magic of faith become as simple as the Wise Men who followed a star to a crib, and as childlike as shepherds who followed a song to its Singer, where old things are made new, where old hearts are gladdened into childhood, where children's hearts are made permanently young, where we crawl out of the web of time back into the womb of eternity, where everything is young because God is life, and life is truth, and truth is love.

"A Child is born." To some He comes on this Christmas Day even in the remorse that follows, "There is no room"; to some He comes when their hearts are saddened by a life that has been taken away, and can be gladdened only by a life that is given; to some He comes when their hearts like conscious mangers cry out, "Lord, I am not worthy"; to others He comes as their study of science reminds them that the only star worth studying is the Star that leads to the Maker of the Stars; to others He comes when their hearts are broken, that He might enter in to heal with wings wider than the world; to others He comes in joy amidst the *Venite Adoremus* of the angels; to others He comes because they are so young they can never remember another Christmas—but to each and every one He comes as if He had never come before in His own sweet way, He the Child who is born, He whose life begins at birth, He, Jesus the Savior, He, Emmanuel, He, Christ at Christ's Mass on Christmas—Merry Christmas!

THE WHOLE CHRIST

DELIVERED ON DECEMBER 30, 1934

LAST year it was my happy privilege to address you on the most beautiful of all subjects: the life of our divine Lord. In a few broad strokes I attempted to fire your hearts with the realization that He was not just a moral reformer, but a merciful Redeemer, and not merely a good man but the infinitely good God. You, of course, realize that that earthly life was lived over nineteen hundred years ago, in a small obscure corner of the earth. Simply because it belongs to the past there is grave danger that we may think it has little relation to the present. Many of us have probably, as practical-minded persons, asked ourselves such questions as these: What possible relation can I, in this twentieth century, have to Him who lived in the first? What influence can His Life of long ago have upon my life at the present? How can any bond of union that I have with Him differ from my relation to Plato or Buddha or Confucius? It is these questions which I hope to answer, with the help of God's grace, in this year's radio course. It need hardly be added that in the choice of such a subject there is only one purpose in mind: to teach the hungry hearts and souls of our land that Christ is the life of their souls, their only solace and their only peace.

Now to plunge into the important question: How does Jesus of Nazareth influence me who am centuries removed from Him by time and thousands of miles by space? The answer is that there are several ways in which any man may influence posterity even long after his death. And the first of these is by teaching.

Anyone who ever wrote or spoke profound truths may echo himself from the grave.

Thanks to their teaching, the wisdom of the Greeks lives amongst us. Plato and Aristotle are enshrined in our universities, and professors talk of them as if they had walked with them through the marketplaces and porches of Athens. Augustine of the fifth century and Aquinas of the thirteenth are made to come from their graves, and by their written word instruct our hearts, minds, and souls in the things of God and men. And who is there who will deny that Washington and Lincoln live beyond their day by their state papers, so full of the finest political traditions of a free people?

Our blessed Lord can influence us in precisely the same way. His words of heavenly wisdom were not allowed to fade away on an evening breeze, but were caught up by his four evangelists— Matthew, Mark, Luke, John—so that all who could read or hear would know the wisdom of One who spoke, not as the Scribes and Pharisees, but as one having authority, even the authority of God. The Scriptures then constitute the first great link between the past and the present, between His earthly life and our modern existence.

But there is a second way in which a character of the past may make himself felt in the present, and that is by example. Any man who has ever had a biographer or who has written the incidents of his own life, may project the force of his personality into the future long after his flesh has crumbled into a heap of moulded dust. The military example of a Caesar or a Napoleon, the saintly life of a Vincent de Paul or a Don Bosco, the daring exploits of a Columbus or a Magellan, can be told and retold a thousand times, and thus become an inspiration and a challenge to saintly and brave men of other times and different climes.

In like manner our Lord can influence our day because He has left us a beautiful example of a holy, moral life that we should follow. We too can be forgiving as He forgave those who crucified Him; we can be gentle as He was gentle to little children, humble as He was before those who would make Him an earthly king, and prayerful as He was in the long vigils on the mountain tops. Countless indeed are the heroic, self-sacrificing, and saintly deeds of our own day, which have had as their inspiration the example of Him who left the heavens to teach us the manner of men God from all eternity wished us to be.

Such are the two ways by which all men and our Lord in particular strike root even centuries after their death, namely, by teaching and example. The pity is that so many believe these are the only two ways for our Lord to stir the hearts and fire the minds of our day. As a matter of fact, if our divine Savior had no other way to project Himself to our day than by the Gospel records of what He said and what He did, then how would He differ from Plato or Confucius, Mohammed or Caesar? They too live in the present by their teaching and by their example. Even grant that His words are more magnetic and His deeds more noble than those of other men, if He has no other way to project Himself than that common to all men, then He is only a man and not God. If our Lord had no other way to energize the hearts and minds than the two ways common to all, then Christianity is only the memory of a man who lived and died; then it is no more worth preserving than any human religion. Modern milk-and-water Christianity regards the life of Christ as nothing more than the life of a good man, and because it bids us look back nineteen hundred years to Israel and Judea, because it merely repeats His words, re-interprets His actions, and recalls His example, as it might do that of Scipio or Aurelius, it has lost its hold on the modern man. If that were all Christianity were, then it should die, for men cannot be influenced long by a mere memory, however noble; it is the curse of a sin-stricken humanity quickly to forget even the finest heritages of the past.

Christianity, fortunately, is something more than a memory, because our Lord is something more than a man. He is true God and true man. Being God He can perpetuate Himself not only by His teaching and His example, which is a means common to all men, but also by a third way which belongs to Him alone, as God; namely by His life. Others may leave their titles, their wealth, their stocks and their bonds, their doctrines and their biographies, but only our Lord can make a last will and testament bequeathing to posterity that which no one else on dying could ever leave—His life and the life of the world. He brought divine life to earth at the crib, but He willed not that that life should be only a temporary visitation of a score and ten years, and a localized experience confined to a few hundred square miles. He willed to diffuse it in time until the consummation of the world, and in space until all the thirsty hearts of earth had drunk of its refreshing draughts. It is of this sublime thought of divine life prolonged and diffused to all men that St. John speaks in the prologue of his Gospel: "of whose fullness we have all received." It is that fullness of the Christ-life beating and throbbing at this very hour in millions of souls which gives flesh and blood to His teaching and His example. No longer is His teaching a cold record written alone on the pages of history, but a teaching bound up with a life in a living mind. No longer is His example an antiquated historical phenomenon but a living force walking before our very eyes.

The life of Christ then is more than a memory of a past. There are really three phases to the complete life of Christ, or the whole Christ: His earthly life, His glorified life, His mystical life.

THE CHRIST

His earthly life covered a space of about thirty-three years, extending from His birth at Nazareth through His public life, Crucifixion, and Resurrection, to His Ascension into heaven, from whence He came. In His glorified life in Heaven, He sits at the right hand of the Father, not only enjoying the eternal repose merited by His glorious triumphs, but also continuing to exercise the power given to Him by His Father to teach, govern, and sanctify men. His mystical life in the Church began on the day of Pentecost when He sent His Spirit upon the Apostles, in order that He might not be external to His Church as an example to be copied, but *internal* with it as a life to be lived.

The complete life of Christ must include these three phases, and without any one of them we know not Christ. Those who consider only the earthly life of Christ develop either a sentimental spirituality or else end by regarding Him only as a good man and a teacher of humanitarian ethics; those who consider Him only in His heavenly life of glory regard Him as an absentee landlord disregarding both His promise to send His Spirit and His abiding interest in the souls whom He came to save.

The whole Christ embraces not only the earthly life in which He redeemed, but also the glorified and mystical life by which He pours out the fruits of Redemption upon the world. For the present it suffices us to know that He is not only our Truth because of His teaching, not only our Way because of His example, but also our Life because our Savior and our Redeemer. His life is not something gone from us, but living amongst us, making our lives livable, hopeful, and glad. Our eyes need not look back to Bethlehem, for the Wise Men and the simple shepherds are still at the feet of Christ. There is nothing past in Him who is eternal. There are no memories of Him who is the "same yesterday, today, and tomorrow." There are no distances from here to Galilee, for He who is divine has pitched His tent in the very center of our hearts and civilization. Why, *Christ is our contemporary*—because He is eternal life.

The years come and go, but He alone abides. Hence I can think of no better way to wish you a happy new year, than to wish you the fullness of that life which is always new, because it measures itself not by years but by Love.

That beautiful theme of eternal life which we begin now at the dawn of the new year will be the burden of these radio discourses until Easter. There is much that remains to be said, but let me conclude with this one thought which, if you think it out in your soul with prayer, will make this year the happiest you ever lived: If it is within man's power to prolong himself through space and time by doctrine and example, why is it not within Christ's power to prolong Himself by His life? If you believe He is God, you must believe this; but if you believe this you must find out where that divine life is, for life is not something vague and undefined like a fog. If that divine life is on this earth, it must be found in some organism, for life on earth is never found divorced from a body. Now where is that Body? Where is the life of Christ? If you will be good enough to listen in next Sunday, I shall tell you.

* * *

THE MYSTICAL BODY

DELIVERED ON JANUARY 6, 1935

LAST Sunday the burden of my discourse was that our Blessed Savior prolongs Himself through space and time and unto this very hour, not only by His doctrine, not only by His example, but principally by His life. Today, with your kind indulgence, I should like to set before you how our Lord continues to live amongst us, just as really and truly as He lived in Galilee and Judea nineteen hundred years ago.

You will recall that when our Lord brought divine life to this earth these nineteen centuries ago, He assumed a human nature from His Blessed Mother, a human nature like unto ours in all things save sin, so that He was in the most exact sense of the words true God and true man. Through the instrumentality of His human nature He did many things, just as we do many things with our arms. In fact St. John tells us that if all the things our Lord did and said were set down "the world itself...would not be able to contain the books that should be written." But this beautiful variety of actions is all reducible to three, for He filled a triple role or office. He was Teacher; He was King; He was Priest. And it was thanks to the body which He assumed from the womb of His Blessed Mother that He was able to make His teaching, His power, and His sanctification visible to men, for the whole plan of the Incarnation was based upon the communication of the divine through the human, the invisible through the visible, and the eternal through the temporal.

But our Lord's earthly life was not long, as we reckon a human life. He completed His Father's business while still in His early thirties. He knew that His footprints would soon fade away from the sands of the seashore and the dust of Jerusalem's streets. He knew furthermore that Peters and Johns of the twentieth century would stand in just as much need of His teaching, His power, and His sanctification, as the Peters and Johns of His own day. Knowing all this, He would therefore not be an architect who lays a foundation and then disappears. He vowed His life to all men at all times and all places, to be their Teacher, their King, and their Priest unto "the consummation of the world."

But how could He be with us as Teacher, King, and Priest to the consummation of the world? He told us how. He said He would be with us in a new body which He would take from humanity as He took His physical body from His Blessed Mother. The new body would not be a physical body, which He was taking to heaven, but rather a social body, like a kingdom or a spiritual corporation.

He went so far as to describe the details of this new body, and He outlined the following characteristics:

Firstly, it would be a living body or organism united to Him as branches are united to the vine, so that His divine life would flow through it as divine life flowed through His physical body. Anyone therefore that would do harm to it would do harm to Him.

Second, this living body would grow like a seed cast into the earth, and although small at first, like the mustard seed, it would grow until it filled the earth.

Third, it would be imperfect in some of the individuals which made it up. There would be good and bad fish, sheep and goats, foolish and wise virgins in it until the final reckoning when the good would be eternally sealed in His body and the wicked rejected.

Fourthly, even though there would be scandals within this body and persecution without, the body would never die, for it was founded on a rock and not even the gates of hell would prevail against it.

Fifthly, membership in that body could be obtained only by being born into it. A man is made a citizen of natural society by being born into it; in like manner a man is made a member of this new spiritual society by being born of the baptismal waters of the Holy Ghost.

Finally, this body in order to be united to Him as branches to vine or as body to head must have a unifying soul or spirit. And so on the night before He died He said to His Apostles that as He and the Father were one, because united by the bond of love, the Holy Spirit, so the new body and He would be one because united by that same Spirit of Love, which He and the Father would send unto it.

Such was the nature of the new body our Lord said He would assume. And He assumed it on Pentecost when He sent the Holy Spirit upon His Apostles. They were the nucleus or germ of His new body, for they had been told that they were to represent Him when He was gone; to stand before princes and governors and speak the truths His Spirit would give them to speak. They were to evangelize the world, because they are His posthumous Self, His prolonged Personality, the scattered reapers of His harvest, the lights kindled as His great Light, the broken syllables of Him who is the Word.

Ten days after His Ascension these frail, weak creatures, as yet full of their individual doubts and ambitions, were lifted into higher unity by the gift of the Holy Ghost, made the branches of

Him the eternal Vine, the living kingdom of Him the heavenly King, and the new body of Him the glorified Christ. In a word, Pentecost was the birthday of the new Body of Christ.

What is this new body which He assumed, and with which He is one because the Spirit makes of Him in Heaven and it on earth one living whole? If I told you it was the Church you would not believe me—not perhaps because you distrust me, but because the truth is so overwhelming. I shall therefore let St. Paul tell you clearly and unmistakably: "His body...is the Church" (Col. 1:24).

Naturally the Church is not His physical body, for that is already in Heaven with the Father. Nor is it a moral body like a nation, or an organization, or a club, because the unity which binds members together in these is merely their corporate will to achieve a common ideal. The unity which binds together the members of the Body of Christ, which is made up of all born into it by baptism, is not their wills, but a superior principle of unity, namely the third Person of God or the Holy Spirit, which is the Spirit of Charity and Love. In order to express that transcendent unearthly unity by which we are all one in Christ, tradition has applied the term mystical, so that the Church is in the proper sense of the term the "Mystical Body of Christ." As the human body is made up of millions of cells and hundreds of organs; as one cell is not another cell, and yet all constitute one body, because governed by one head and unified by one soul; so in the Mystical Body of Christ there are millions and millions of members, and hundreds of officers; and in it the layman is not the priest, as the foot is not the hand, and the cardinal is not the missionary, as one organ is not another; yet they all coalesce into one living body, because governed by the invisible head, Christ, and vivified by the one soul which is the Holy Spirit of God.

The Church then is the Body of Christ. But what does He do with this new Body? Our Lord in heaven does the same three things with it that He did with His individual human nature taken from Mary; namely, through its instrumentality, He teaches because He is its teacher, He governs because He is its king, He sanctifies because He is its priest. He was teacher, but He gave the power to His new Body: "As the Father hath sent me, I also send you"; "Going therefore teach ye all nations"; and "He that heareth you, heareth me; and he that despiseth you, despiseth me." Certainly, if these words mean anything, they mean that just as He once taught through His visible form as man, so now He continues to teach through His new body, the Church, the truth forever being not the Church's but His, and therefore infallible.

He was king with power in heaven and earth. This office He gave to His new Body: "All power is given to me in heaven and in earth. My power I give unto you: Whatsoever thou shalt bind upon earth, it shall be bound also in heaven: and whatsoever thou shalt loose on earth, it shall be loosed also in heaven." These words mean that He, as He was formerly king in His individual, physical manhood, so now He is king through His new manhood the Church, the power being not the Church's but His, and therefore divine.

He was priest, who came to give His life for the redemption of many. This office He gave to His new body: "Baptize them in the name of the Father, and of the Son, and of the Holy Ghost." "Do this for a commemoration of me." "Whose sins you shall forgive they are forgiven them; and whose sins you shall retain, they are retained." Again the meaning is unmistakable—as He had sanctified souls and offered His own Body and Blood to His heavenly Father, so now He was communicating that power to His Mystical Body, the sanctification forever being not the Church's but His, and therefore divine.

Is this a new and strange doctrine that Christ is living today in His Church as really and truly as He lived in His physical nature nineteen hundred years ago? For those who might doubt it let them recall the conversion of Saint Paul. This fiery Hebrew of the Hebrews grew up with an unholy hatred of Christ and things Christian. His first appearance is in that role of hatred when as Saul, he holds the garments of those who stoned Stephen the first Christian martyr. Saul was not just a bigot. He was a learned man, trained under Gamaliel, and so powerful a disputant that the early Christians must often have wondered who they could get to refute him. In the providence of God it was reserved that a Paul should refute a Saul. One day he set out on a journey for Damascus, authorized by letters to seize the Christians of that city, bind them, and bring them back to Jerusalem. Breathing out hatred against the Lord he sets out to persecute the infant Church of Damascus. The time is only a few years after the Resurrection and Ascension of our divine Savior. While on this journey, suddenly a great light shines about him, he falls to the ground, and a voice arouses him like a bursting sea, saying: "Saul, Saul, why persecutest thou me?" The heat of the oriental sun gave him strength enough to speak, and nothingness dared ask the name of Omnipotence: "Who art thou, Lord?" And He answered: "I am Jesus whom thou persecutest."

Saul was striking the Church in the city of Damascus in exactly the same way that the government of Mexico persecutes the Church of Mexico—and the Voice from heaven says: "Saul, Saul, why persecutest thou me?" Christ and the Church—are they one and the same? Precisely—the Church *is* Christ.

THE CHRIST

The risen Christ, only four or five years after He left this earth, breaks open heaven in order to declare to Saul and the world that the Church is His Body; that in striking that body, Saul struck its Head, Christ; that He and the Church were one Person; that just as the tongue speaks when the foot is stepped on, so when His body, the Church, is persecuted it is the Head, Christ, who arises to speak.

On Holy Thursday night when a soldier in the hall of the High Priest struck our Lord with a mailed fist He asked: "If I have spoken evil, give testimony of the evil; but if well, why strikest thou me?" And now Christ in His glory, who has incorporated unto Himself His new body the Church, still cries out when that body is struck: "Why persecutest thou me?" What does all this mean, but that Calvary may be prolonged even beyond Jerusalem's walls, and the life of Christ in His Church extended beyond the sands of a Galilean seashore and the memorial of an upper room? No wonder the transformed Saul, Saint Paul, understood so well the nature of the Church. He knew Christ, too, as well as the other Apostles, for he too had touched His body.

How far removed is this doctrine of the Church from those who would accuse the Church of standing between Christ and us. How often we hear it said: "I do not want an organization between Christ and me"; or, "True religion consists in union with Jesus of Nazareth without priest, or prelate, or sacrament." Anyone who understands the Scriptures will see that the Church does not stand between Christ and me. The Church is Christ. It no more stands between Christ and me than His feet stood between Magdalene and His forgiveness, or His hand stood between the little children and His blessing, or His breast stood between John and the secrets of the Sacred Heart. The Church no more stands between the divine life of Christ and my soul than His physical body stands between me and His divinity. It is through His human body that He comes to me in His individual life; it is through His Mystical Body that He comes to me in His corporate life. Christ is the Church. Her real, inner self, is His body permeated through and through with His redemptive life. We who are members of His Mystical Body are not merely imitators of Christ; we are not merely lovers of His doctrine—we are more. Why, we are the cells in that very body which is Christ!

Any suggestion therefore of the Church being an obstacle to our union with Christ is based upon a misunderstanding of the meaning and beauty of the Incarnation of our Lord. For just as our Lord lived a physical life two thousand years ago in a body taken from Mary, so now He lives a mystical life in a body drawn from the womb of humanity. To the eyes of every member of that Church the Eternal Galilean relives the events and crises of His life in Judea and Galilee. The written Gospel is the record of His historical life. The Church is the living Gospel and record of His present life.

The Church is that without which Christ would be limited and imperfect. Were it not for His Mystical Body where would Christ find lips with which to say forgiveness to penitent thieves? If it were not for this Body where would He find hands to lay on little children, feet to receive the ointment of other Magdalenes, and a breast to receive the embrace of other Johns? Were it not for this Body where would Christ find a visible head to articulate His voice and draw all souls into the unity of one Lord, one faith, one baptism?

How else could He as the Incarnate God console other widows than those of Naim, visit other friends than those of Bethany, attend other nuptials than those of Cana, call other apostles than those of a lake, convert other women than those of Samaria, and other men than the centurions of Calvary; how could He the God-man show meekness to other soldiers, patience to other timid disciples, love for other publicans, friendliness to other Judases, forgiveness to other malefactors, devotion to other Johns, affection to other Marys, wisdom to other Doctors of the Law—except through another body with the feet of which He could step from Jerusalem to the world, with the lips of which He could speak to us who call ourselves modern? The Upper Room is in our cities, as with other hands we lift to His Father the chalice of His Blood shed for the redemption of many; Carpharnaum is at the border of all our waters as He calls to Himself other fishers of men; Nazareth is at Lourdes as Mary Immaculate mothers her new children, brothers of Christ and sons of the Heavenly Father. Rather, Christ is at our very door. If we do not see Christ, living in His Mystical Body the Church today, then we would not have believed Him divine if we had seen Him in His physical Body in Galilee. If we miss Him, it will be not because He is too far away, but because He is too close.

THE VICAR OF CHRIST

DELIVERED ON JANUARY 13, 1935

LAST Sunday I told you how Christ, who is gloriously reigning in heaven, is the Head of His Mystical Body which is the Church, and how the unity existing between Christ and the Church is like the unity of the head and the body, the vine and the branches. A very practical problem confronting us today is this: How will men know where to find the Church of the Body of Christ? Once our Lord was in heaven, would it not be natural for each of the conflicting groups to say that it was the one body of Christ?

Our blessed Lord did not leave this question unanswered. He came on earth to leave us truth and it is natural that He should not only preserve it, but should also leave some definite mark of identification. The sign He left was the sign of all living things. Now what is the sign of a living organism if it be not the head, which is the source of the movements of the whole body? In the organic order the head is the symbol of the unity of life. Legs and arms, muscles and sinews, may be amputated without necessarily destroying the unity of life, but the cutting off of the head, the center of unity, means the end of life. In the social order likewise we know a club, or a group, or a society, or a nation to be one because of its head—its president, its king, or its ruler. In the psychological order the head subsumes all the activities of body and mind in the primacy of the personal pronoun "I." Life then by its very nature expresses its unity in a center of reference, in a brain, in a head, in a primacy of personality.

Now if the life of Christ and His Church is one, the obvious way in which we might expect Christ to identify His Body after His Ascension would be a visible head or a primate. He was its invisible Head, but that would not prevent Him from leaving a visible representative of His headship, any more than His Godhead prevented Him from using men as the preachers of His word, water as the channel of His regenerative grace, and bread as the means for communicating His eternal life. What we should therefore expect Christ to do, in the very nature of things, is what He actually did. He appointed a visible head for His body as the symbol of His oneness with both.

Of course, He might have done otherwise for there are two other possible forms of Church government than the one He chose. Before founding a monarchical government for His Church He considered the two other plans, namely, the democratic and the aristocratic.

The democratic form of Church government contends that God should make each individual his own supreme authority, allowing him either to interpret the Scriptures privately as he sees fit, or else free to interpret his own religious experiences without any dictation from without, which is tantamount to a negation of his personality.

The second possible form of Church government is the aristocratic in which a select group, a council, a federation, a parliament, or the representatives of different religious bodies themselves, determine, insofar as is possible, the beliefs, worship, and creeds of those under them. National churches which are subject to a parliament are typical of this form of Church government.

The form our Lord chose was neither of these, but what might be called the monarchical. In this form the head, who is the sign of the unity of the body, exercises universal and immediate jurisdiction over the whole Church and every member of it. This power of jurisdiction is not conferred upon him by a council, but given immediately by God, a further assurance of the oneness of Christ and His Church.

Our blessed Lord chose the third or monarchical form, but He did not choose it until He had eliminated the other two faulty plans of His creatures.

The important matter was discussed about the middle of His public career. The scene was the city of Caesarea-Phillippi. In that pagan spot, He, the Lord and Master of the world, stopped to ask a question, the true answer to which would put an end to paganism if men would but heed it. The question was the most important one He ever asked in His life and startled them all into a new birth of faith.

The question He asked was about His inmost nature, for unless men knew that under that human nature was beating the very life of God, they could never know the secrets the divine Heart had for men; unless they knew He was God they could never know the divinity of the Church He came to establish as His Body. And so He asked: "Whom do men say that the Son of man is?" Note that it was an appeal to the democratic form of church government: Whom do men say that I am? That is, whom do men, individually interpreting their own experiences or constituting themselves as individual judges of my revealed word, or setting themselves up as the last court of appeal, whom do they say that I am?

The answer was the answer of confusion. Men had arrived at various conclusions; what else could they arrive at? "Some [say that you are] John the Baptist, and other some Elias, and others Jeremias, or one of the prophets." All rudimentary guesses of the poor and ignorant. No certainty! No agreement! No unity so dear to the heart of God! Leave the secret of His nature to individuals and the responses are bound to be contradictory, contrary, and confusing, one man denying what another has said! The answers were so stupidly incongruous to His divine nature, to His love of truth, that He brought to it the withering scorn of His silence—*the democratic principle would not do.*

And so He passes on to the aristocratic. He no longer asks the mob. He turns to the aristocrats, the elders, the chosen twelve, to those who represent the people He serves, those who as a group make up His select council, his federation, his parliament, and says to them: "But whom do *you* say that I am?"—*you,* the aristocrats, not *men* now, but *you...*

And the twelve do not answer. Why are they silent? Because perhaps if they all spoke at once there would only be confusion of tongues; because also, perhaps, if one spoke for the others they would have asked who gave him authority to speak; silence, too, perhaps because each one was hoping to be supreme, for they more than once had been found disputing which was the greater amongst them; silence perhaps because they knew down deep in their hearts that if the truth of the Church was to be merely belief of the majority then God's truth would not be absolute, but subject to the play of human passion, the chance grouping of worldly opinions, and the majority vote of a council. The aristocratic form was a failure too. There is no authority, there is no head, there is therefore no unity.

The democratic and aristocratic forms of church government which men would have suggested to God as the plan for His Church have been eliminated. There remains now but one other—the monarchical, which focused its expression in Peter.

Peter now steps forward, not because the apostles asked him

to do so, not because he was personally moved to do so as an individual, but because there came to him a great light, a light that was almost too great for him, a light that made him first for eternity, a light not kindled by the sparks of his own reason, but coming from above like the sun that shone upon his head. An interior spirit, an inward light, a heavenly revelation gave him the answer to the question of the Master and expressed itself in a testimony which a moment before he would have believed impossible: "Thou art Christ, the Son of the living God."

Peter knew who He was. He was not John the Baptist. He was not Elias. He was the One to whom the Gentile and Jewish world had been expectantly looking for these past forty centuries. He was Emmanuel, God-with-us! The Son of the Living God! Jesus Christ, true God and true Man!

The Apostles did not tell Peter who Christ was. He did not even tell himself at that moment. The moment he said it he was certain he had divine assistance. It was only by some sudden illumination of his mind that he knew, and our Lord assured him it was so: "Blessed art thou, Simon Bar-Jona, for flesh and blood hath not revealed it to thee, but my Father who is in heaven."

Here the plan of Christ's visible kingdom on earth becomes complete. One man, Peter, without the consent of the others, without their authority, but with divine assistance, speaks in the name of all, that Christ is God. Our Lord seized upon it immediately to make him the visible sign of the unity of Him and His Church: "Thou art Peter; and upon this rock I will build my church, and the gates of hell shall not prevail against it. And I will give to thee the keys of the kingdom of heaven. And whatsoever thou shalt bind upon earth, it shall be bound also in heaven: and whatsoever thou shalt loose on earth, it shall be loosed also in heaven."

The meaning of the words was unmistakable. The Church which was His Body would be one with Him because it would have a visible head—not only a head with the primacy of honor but with the very primacy of jurisdiction. No detail was left undetermined concerning the nature of that jurisdiction. Our Lord spoke of the foundation of His Church, about the outside of His Church, and about the inside of His Church, and all three revolved about one man. The foundation is the rock which is Peter; the door to the edifice from the outside is to be opened by keys, and these keys are suspended from the cincture of the fisherman Peter; and once on the inside, the same rock and key-bearer has the power to bind and loose, to seal and unseal consciences even for registry in the book of life.

The question of how will men know the Body of Christ which is His Church was now answered.

The sign was given; the identification marks were sealed; the brand was stamped. Men would know the Body of Christ, and the union of Christ and His Church, by the sign of all life, namely, by its head. They might not accept it; they might disbelieve or reject it—but the sign was there for those who would read it. Mankind would know His Body was one because it had one head, whose authority came not from below as a gift of men, but from above as a revelation of God. As a nation is one because it has one executive, as a club is one because it has one president, as a body is one because it has one head, so too the Church is one because its head is one. That is why there arose from primitive Christians a cry which has been echoed to our own day: "*Ubi Petrus ibi Ecclesia*"—"Wherever Peter is, there is the Church." Not indeed that Peter is a head apart from Christ, but only that he is one authority with Him. He is merely the visible representation, the concrete symbol, the vicar of the Sender among the sent, the foundation stone conjoined with the corner stone which is the invisible Christ; or as our Lord put it after the Resurrection, Peter was to feed His lambs and feed His sheep. This meant more clearly than ever that Christ did not lose His sheep or His lambs, nor did He relinquish power over them, but only that He communicated this power to shepherd His flock and shepherd His shepherds to His visible shepherd, His visible head, the sign of the unity of His Church—Peter the Rock.

This great truth of the natural and supernatural order never dawns on one with such overwhelming force and peaceful consolation as when one enters the great basilica of St. Peter's in the city made eternal not because the Roman eagles screamed their might of arms across a world, but because a fisherman went there to die. Under the great dome, the largest thing man ever threw against the vault of the heaven's blue, rests the tomb of Christ's first vicar and key-bearer, Peter. That humble, ignorant, all-so-human laborer, who earned his living beside the waters of the Galilean lake, and who earned his crown by the waters of Tiber's river, had his abode shifted from a crude Capharnaum cottage to the grandest of Rome's temples, to be ever near the Christ on the altar and his successor in the Vatican.

It is impossible for any loyal member of Christ's Mystical Body to describe the emotions that surge through his soul and testify to their own inarticulateness in tears, when he passes from that tomb of the dead Simon Bar-Jona to the living Peter of the Vatican. He is a man like unto us, subject to all our weakness and frailties, and as subject to error in human things as anyone in the world. His family name we know: it is Ratti; and yet to us who have the faith it is Peter. The very first moment our Lord looked upon His first Vicar He said to him: "Thou art Simon the son of Jona: thou shalt be called Cephas, which is interpreted

Peter." As much as to say: "Leave off thy name of earth; take on the name of eternity." And that distinction which Christ Himself made between the man and his office, we make as we kneel before the saintly man in white: "Thou art called Ratti; henceforth thou shalt be called Peter."

To us, then, Pius XI is Peter, appointed by Christ. He is the Vicar of Christ, the visible embodiment of the Redeemer of the world, the sign of the unity of Christ and His Body, the shepherd of Christ's sheep, the man in whom as an individual virtue might fail and charity grow cold, but in whom as the representative of Christ faith will never fail—for Christ has prayed: "I have prayed for thee that thy faith fail not," and Christ's prayers are always heard. He calls himself the "servant of the servants of God," but to us he is called by the dearest term of all: "Holy Father."

As we kneel for the blessing of that father of fathers and have our souls sealed with the triune seal of the Trinity which Christ commanded Peter and His Apostles to teach the world, we arise to make our way back to the tomb of Peter, every step testifying to a chain of two hundred and fifty-three links which holds the Peter of today to the Peter of yesterday. And as our eyes glance up to that dome above the tomb, even that seems to seal the certainty of our faith in the continuity of Caesarea-Phillipi and Rome, as we read in gigantic letters of gold the words Christ spoke to Peter: "Thou art Peter; and upon this rock I will build my Church, and the gates of hell shall not prevail against it."

Glancing now from that dome to the tomb below, we seem to catch the beautiful significance of the death of Peter. Our Lord told him he would be crucified and when the moment came for him to surrender his life, on the very spot where his Church now stands, he begged his executioners to crucify him upside down, as if unworthy to die as his Master had died. His Lord was crucified head upwards as if to signify that He, Christ the invisible Head, was to be in heaven.

But Peter asked to be crucified head downwards, for as the visible rock and foundation stone of the Church, he was to be laid like all foundation stones—on the earth, in order that we, the other living stones, might build upon him as the immutable rock, and compacted together in the bonds of faith, hope, and charity, for the salvation of souls and the glory of God.

THE SOUL OF THE CHURCH

DELIVERED ON JANUARY 20, 1935

THE Church is the Body of Christ. The Body is constituted of the millions of individuals who have been incorporated to it by Baptism under the government of the invisible Head, Christ and the visible Head, the Vicar of Christ on earth. Thus we have progressed in our study of the Church. Today we go one step further. A body and a head are not sufficient to constitute the Mystical Christ as the Church. The Church must also have a soul as the principle of its life and its unity. That soul is the Holy Ghost. Such is the idea I would lay before your minds today.

In order that you may properly understand the role the Holy Ghost, the Third Person of the Blessed Trinity, plays in the Church, try to picture the Apostles and the faithful on earth during the ten days after the Ascension of our Lord into heaven. The Church then existed in its raw material—its great arteries had been formed, its head had been named, its members were called, but it still lacked a soul. The condition of the Church at this time may be imperfectly likened to America before the drawing up of the Declaration of Independence. The Dutch, the English, the French, the Irish, the Scotch, and the other nationalities were scattered up and down the Atlantic seaboard, but there was no common bond or spirit holding them together. They needed unity—a soul to make them one. That spark came in the Declaration of Independence which fired them with the spirit of free-born American people. The Church was somewhat in this position. The Apostles and disciples and the faithful were still separate individuals; they needed a soul to make them one. But here the analogy breaks down. The spirit which was to make the members of the Church one was different from the spirit which made America one.

The condition of the Church can be represented better by the analogy of life. The members were like the elements in a chemical laboratory, capable of being part of a body, and yet not a body because lacking a soul. We know up to one hundred percent the chemicals which enter into the constitution of a human body, and yet with all our superior knowledge of chemistry, we cannot make a body in our laboratories. Why? Because we lack the power to give a unifying principle, a soul, to those chemicals which will make them mutually coalesce into that new emergent which we call life. Now the Apostles were like the chemicals in a laboratory; they were individuals, each with his own outlook on life, each with his doubts, his uncertainties, his points of view. They could not give themselves unity any more than chemicals can make life. The permanent union of their minds was impossible without a certitude from on high, for life is not a push from below, but a gift from above. They needed a soul, a spirit, a vivifying, unifying principle which would make the cells of the Mystical Body cohere in the unity of a headship under Christ, and this vivifying, unifying spirit did not come until the day of Pentecost.

The Apostles knew the Spirit would come to them; they never would forget the beautiful way which our Lord promised His spirit the night before He died: "I have yet many things to say to you but you cannot bear them now. But when he, the Spirit of truth, is come, he will teach you all truth." "And I will ask the Father, and he shall give you another Paraclete, that he may abide with you for ever. The Spirit of truth, whom the world cannot receive, because it seeth him not, nor knoweth him; but you shall know him; because he shall abide with you, and shall be in you." "I tell you the truth: it is expedient to you that I go: for if I go not, the Paraclete will not come to you; but if I go, I will send him to you."

This was only a promise of the Spirit that was to come. But our Lord keeps His promises. Accordingly, ten days after the Ascension, the Apostles with Peter as their head were in solitude in the Cenacle where the Savior had instituted the Eucharist and appeared to doubting Thomas: "And suddenly there came a sound from heaven, as of a mighty wind coming, and it filled the whole house where they were sitting. And there appeared to them parted tongues as it were of fire, and it sat upon every one of them, and they were all filled with the Holy Ghost."

In the fiery glow of that Pentecostal gift the individuals, the cells of the Mystical Body, like the bones in the vision of Ezechiel, were drawn together into a living body, animated by the eternal Spirit of the Third Person of the Blessed Trinity. The scattered rays now emerged into the light of the world. All they had dimly guessed at and faintly perceived now became absolute certainty in the glow of the Pentecostal fire, as they saw the continuity of Nazareth and the Cenacle: for as Christ had taken His physical body from the womb of the Virgin Mary overshadowed by the Holy Ghost, so now was Christ taking from the womb of humanity His Mystical Body overshadowed by the Pentecostal Spirit. The Church was now created in the strictest sense of the term; it had its head, Christ; its soul, the Holy Spirit; and its body, which we are.

Pentecost is the explanation of the words of our Lord that the Church would exist all days even to the consummation of the world. Organization does not explain its enduring power over the centuries. Nations have had greater organization; they have even had armies to ensure obedience to commands, and yet these powerful nations passed away, leaving not a trace behind. Where then find the source of the unfailing life of the Church? The answer is: The Church is not an organization; it is an organism, a divine-human organism modelled upon the Incarnation and infused with the eternal Spirit of God. A human organism remains the same throughout the vicissitudes of life, the changing of bodily cells, the shock of environment, the process of learning, simply because the human organism is infused with an immortal soul. In like manner the Church.

Organization has nothing to do with this marvelous vitality of the Church, nor has any other human explanation. If the Church were left to its human elements it would have perished long ago. The secret of her immortal life is her eternal spirit which cannot be destroyed by the world any more than the soul of an infant can be destroyed. Hence in the face of the force of violence the Spirit manifests the immortality of her being; against the force of idea the Spirit shows the immortality of her ideas; and against the force of passion the Spirit shows the immortality of her love.

If there is any picture which adequately describes the Church in time, it is that of a person living throughout the cataclysms and revolutions, the progress and the unfolding of the centuries. A man who is fifty today is the same identical person as always despite the changes in his bodily life and the historic upheavals of our times. He can say: I saw mankind exalt itself to a god in the pre-war period; I saw that same humanity prove it was not a god but only a beast in the battlefields of the World War; I saw it settle down to a false peace without ever learning the lesson that it cannot survive without God. In like manner the Church

is an abiding Person through nineteen centuries. The only difference between her now and then is the difference between
the acorn and the oak, the mustard seed and the great tree. Her
members have come and gone, like the cells in a human body,
but her Spirit has remained one and the same. And since it is the
Spirit which makes the Body, the Church which is the Mystical
Body of Christ has been contemporaneous with the centuries.
When therefore we in this twentieth century wish to know about
Christ, about His early Church, about history, we go not only
to the dusty records but to the living Church, which says to us:
"I lived with Christ. I saw His Mother and I know her to be a
Virgin and the loveliest and purest of all women in heaven or
on earth. I saw Christ at Caesarea-Phillippi when after changing Simon's name to Rock He told him he was the rock upon
which the Church would be built and on which it would endure
unto the consummation of the world. I saw Christ hanging on
a cross and I saw Him rise from His tomb; I saw Magdalene
rush to His feet; I saw the angels clad in white beside the great
stone; I was in the Cenacle room when doubting Thomas put
fingers into His hands; I was on Olivet when He ascended into
heaven and promised to send His Spirit to the Apostles to make
them the foundation of His new Mystical Body on earth. I was
at the stoning of Stephen, saw Saul hold the garments of those
who slew him, and later I heard Saul, as Paul, preach Christ
and Him crucified; I witnessed the beheading of Paul in Rome
and with my very eyes saw tens of thousands of martyrs crimson the sands with their blood rather than deny the faith Peter
and Paul had preached unto them; I was living when Boniface
was sent to Germany, when Augustine went to England, Cyril
and Methodius to the Poles, and Patrick to Ireland; in the ninth
century I recall seeing Charlemagne crowned as king in matters

temporal, as Peter's vicar was recognized as supreme in matters spiritual; in the thirteenth century I saw the great stones cry out in tribute to me and burst into Gothic cathedrals; in the shadows of those same walls I saw great cathedrals of thought arise in the prose of Aquinas and Bonaventure, and in the poetry of Dante; in the sixteenth century I saw my children, softened by the spirit of the world, leave the Father's house and reform the faith instead of reforming discipline, which would have brought them back again into my embrace; in the last century and at the beginning of this, I heard the world say it could not accept me because I was behind the times. I do change. I have adapted myself to every form of government the world has ever known; I have lived with Caesars and kings, tyrants and dictators, parliaments and presidents, monarchies and republics. I have welcomed every advance of science, and were it not for me the great records of the pagan world would not have been preserved. It is true I have not changed my doctrine, but that is because the 'doctrine is not mine but his that sent me.' I change my garments which belong to time but not my Spirit which belongs to eternity. In the course of my long life, I have seen so many modern ideas become unmodern, that I know I shall live to chant a requiem over the modern ideas of this day as I chanted it over the modern ideas of the last century. Last year I celebrated the nineteen hundredth anniversary of the death of my Redeemer and yet I am no older now than then, for my Spirit is eternal and the eternal never ages. I am the abiding Personage of the centuries. I am the contemporary of all ages. I am one because I have the same soul I had in the beginning; I am holy because that soul is the Spirit of Holiness; I am catholic because that Spirit pervades every living cell of my Body; I am apostolic because identical with Nazareth, Galilee, and Jerusalem. I shall grow weak when my members become rich and cease to pray, but I shall never die. I shall be persecuted as I am persecuted now in Spain and Mexico and Russia; I shall be crucified as I was on Calvary, but I shall rise again, and finally when time shall be no more, and I shall have grown to my full stature, then shall I be taken into heaven as the bride of my Head, Christ, where the celestial nuptials shall be celebrated and God shall be all in all, because His Spirit is Love and Love is Heaven."

Attacks upon the Church will make it more difficult, not for the Church but for the world. Violence against the Mystical Body will only make the earth a more terrible place to live in; it will turn it into a Good Friday Jerusalem, where men, like frightened birds, will fly from the wrath they have pulled down upon themselves; it will make it more difficult for men to see the light thrown from her resplendent body; it will make it more difficult for men to be honest, for marriage to be happy, for children to be loving, for the aged to be hopeful. Persecution will not destroy her divinity, simply because she is divine; it will not kill the Mystical Christ for He has the power to lay down His life and take it up again; it will not weaken her whose love increases with each new vision of the cross, it will not drain the sacraments of their divine life; it will not empty heaven of angels and saints; it will not scale the parapets of eternity; it will not dethrone God. It will only lay waste the earth.

SCANDALS IN THE MYSTICAL BODY

DELIVERED ON JANUARY 27, 1935

THUS far we have spoken of the Church as an *ideal.* The Risen Christ at the right hand of the Father is the head; we the baptized members are the body; and the Holy Spirit of Truth, the Third Person of the Blessed Trinity, is the soul.

But in fact does the Church always reveal that ideal? The world has asked these questions a thousand times: How dare you say that the successor of Peter is the Vicar of Christ? Do not the sinful lives of men who have sat in the chair of Peter prove that they are not infallible? How can anyone be infallible who is a sinner? Do you mean to say that a wicked man like Alexander VI, who was a sinner, could be the infallible Vicar of Jesus Christ? Furthermore, is it not almost blasphemy to say that you Catholics, many of whom have been guilty of grave scandals, murders, political intrigues, dishonesty, and shameful sin, constitute the Body of Christ, and then against bad Catholics; or first, would you dare assert that they were part of the Body of the all-holy Christ? How could He who is pure have a Body which is soiled?

Despite these seemingly strong objections we still believe that the Holy Father is the Vicar of Christ, and the Church is the Body of Christ. I will consider first the objections against the Vicars of Christ, and then against bad Catholics, or first against the Head of the Church and then against its Body.

The root of error on this subject is that the enemies of the Papacy fail to make a distinction between *infallibility* and *impeccability*. Infallibility means freedom from error, impeccability means freedom from sin. Hence this question arises: When our Lord conferred primacy on Peter and his successors did he make them infallible or impeccable? The Gospels themselves make the distinction. Peter made the confession of our Lord's divinity, whereupon our Lord made him the Rock of His Church with the guarantee that the gates of error would never prevail against it.

Immediately after this promise of freedom from error and guarantee of faith, our blessed Lord tells His Apostles that He must "go to Jerusalem, and suffer many things from the ancients and scribes and chief priests, and be put to death."

Poor, weak, human Peter, who was evidently puffed with pride because he had been made the Rock of the Church, was yet to learn the limitations of his gift. Like a boy given authority and anxious to exercise it, Peter now takes our Lord aside, in the language of the Gospel "to rebuke him," saying: "Lord, be it far from thee, this shall not be unto thee."

Whereupon our Lord, whose back was to Peter, turned around and said to Peter: "Go behind me, Satan, thou art a scandal unto me: because thou savourest not the things that are of God, but the things that are of men."

A moment before Peter was called the Rock; now he is called Satan. I think not that the divine Mind had so quickly changed. Our Lord did not take back the gift of primacy, for He re-emphasized it again after His Resurrection. He was just driving home to Peter the distinction between the office and its man, between infallibility and impeccability, between freedom from error and freedom from sin. In so many words our Lord was telling him: "As Peter, the Rock upon which I build My Church, whenever you speak with the assistance of heaven you shall be preserved from error, but as Simon, son of John, as a *man*, you are so weak, so human, so apt to be sinful, that you may become even like unto Satan. In your office you are infallible; as a man, you are peccable." Most of us, too, who examine our relations with our fellow men are conscious of this distinction our Lord made at Caesarea-Phillipi. If an officer of the law holds up his hand and orders you to stop in traffic, you do so. And why? Because he is the representative of law and order. And you would do so even though you knew that as a private citizen the traffic officer was known to beat his wife. In other words you make a distinction between the office and the man. God thus permitted the fall of Peter immediately after the gift of primacy to remind him and all his successors that what he received as Peter was not his as Simon; that infallibility would belong necessarily to his office, but virtue would have to be acquired by his own merit; infallibility would come from God, saintliness would have to come from himself.

Admitting then the weakness of the man, because he is himself, and the power of the office, because that is Christ's, does history justify the emphasis the enemies of the Church have placed upon her failing Peters? To read some histories one would think the Papacy was nothing but a scarlet river of blood. Scandals have the unfortunate quality of absorbing attention. A murderer receives more space in our newspapers than a sacrificing mother. Saints never make the headlines. It is generally safe to say that those who know everything about the two or three bad successors of Peter know nothing at all about the other two hundred and fifty good ones. How true it is that "the evil men do lives after them; the good is oft interred with their bones." The wickedness of one man in authority is allowed to obscure a million saints.

But why not put all things in due proportion? How many who dwell on the Papacy for thirty years during the Renaissance ever dwell on the history of the Papacy for the other hundreds and hundreds of years? How many of those who exploit the bad two or three, ever admit that of the first thirty-three successors of Peter, thirty were martyrs for their faith and the other three exiled for it? How many of those who dwell on the bad example of two or three will know or ever admit that of the two hundred and fifty-three successors of St. Peter eighty-three have been canonized for their heroic virtue, and that over fifty were chosen over the protest of their own unworthiness for such a high office? Anyone who attacks such a long line of martyrs, saints, and scholars must be mighty certain of his own sinlessness to lay his hand on the two or three who revealed the human side of their office. If they who attack are holy, pure, and undefiled—and I wonder how many are—let them pick up their stones. For it is the privilege only of those without sin to cast the first stone. But if they are not above reproach, then let them leave their judgment to God.

Now let us consider the objection against like scandals of the members of His Mystical Body. As Christ never promised that His visible Head would always be a saint, neither did He promise that the members of His Mystical Body would all be saints. Sacred Scripture nowhere guarantees that those who, called to intimate union with God, would all be saints. There were eight in the ark and one was a reprobate; there were twelve tribes and one was rejected for the final sealing; there were twelve apostles and one of them was a devil; there were seventy-two disciples and some walked no more with Christ; there were seven deacons and one of them was a heretic. The Kingdom of God on earth, our blessed Lord assured us, would be made up of foolish virgins as well as wise virgins, of cockle as well as wheat, of bad fish as well as good, and the final rejection of the bad would not take place until the end of time.

In ideal then the Church would always be the "immaculate spouse" of Christ, but that ideal would never be fully realized here below. The world is full of half-completed Gothic cathedrals, of half-written epics, and of unfinished symphonies, and in the Church our Lord Himself told us: "Scandals must come." It is rather natural, too, for them to come when one remembers that the graces of God are communicated through "frail vessels," where mediocrity is the nemesis, genius the rarity, and saints the exception.

Quite apart from the divine warrant that such failings are to be expected, does it not seem to be implied in the very nature of the Mystical Body? In the Incarnation our Lord assumed a physical body, a human nature, like unto ours in all things save sin. The remarkable thing about the assumption of that physical body from the womb of the Blessed Mother was that He, though God, did not dispense that body from the physical imperfections of all human bodies. He was subject to fatigue and thirst when He rested at Jacob's well; He was subject to grief when He wept at the grave of Lazarus; He was subject to a bloody sweat when He bowed down to the Father's will in Gethsemane's garden; and He was subject to pain, anguish, pierced hands and feet, torn body, and bruised brow in what He called the "scandal" of His life—the Crucifixion.

Is it not natural then to expect that in assuming a mystical body, which we are, that He would permit this body to be subject to mystical and moral weakness; such as loss of faith, sin, scandals, heresies, schisms, and sacrileges? And why, when these things do happen, should we deny that the Mystical Body is divine in its inmost nature, any more than we should deny He was divine because of the weakness of His own physical body. The Crucifixion did not obscure His divinity; then why should scandals do so when we find them, as He foretold, in His Mystical Body? But the scandals or sins of a few members do not affect the intrinsic sanctity of the Church. Because one's hands are dirty, the whole body is not polluted. The scandals, sins, and imperfections of the members of the Church no more destroy its substantial holiness than the Crucifixion destroyed the substantial wholeness of Christ's physical body.

Hence it is no great objection against the Mystical Body to urge that some Catholics are bad. The Church no more expected to have perfect Catholics than our Lord expected to have perfect Apostles. Catholics may be bad, but that does not prove Catholicism is wicked, any more than a few bigots prove America is bigoted. If the Catholics are bad, it is not because they are Catholics; it is because they are *not*. Faith increases their responsibility, but it does not force obedience; it increases blame, but it does not prevent sin.

Why is it that the world is always so scandalized at a scandal in the Church? Why does it always blame a bad Catholic more than it blames a bad Mohammedan, if it is not because it expects so much more of the Catholic? Any fallen-away Catholic whose name is quoted as a by-word of sin, and who is supposed to be an argument against the Church, is really a strong Catholic credential. The seriousness of any fall depends on the height from which one has fallen, and since one can fall from no greater height than union with Christ in His Mystical Body, the fall is accordingly greater. Nowhere does evil become so visible as when contrasted with the ideal. The very horror the world expresses at the fall of a Catholic is the measure of the high virtue it expects of him.

Looking at the Church now from another point of view, would not those who object to her because her members are not all holy, be just as scandalized if she were all they wanted her to be? Suppose every Vicar of Christ was a saint; suppose every member of His Mystical Body was another St. John the Baptist or another St. Theresa. Would not her very perfection accuse and condemn those who were outside? Too high an ideal often repels rather than attracts. She would be so saintly that she would no longer allure ordinary mortals. She might, even appear to struggling souls as a terrible Puritan, easily scandalized at our failings, who might shrink from having her garments touched by sinners like ourselves. Where then would faith be for those who doubted? Where would hope be for those who were unholy? Where would charity be for those who were in sin? No, a perfect Church would be a stumbling-block. Then, instead of men being scandalized at her, she would be scandalized at men—which would be far worse.

Our Lord did not make His earthly life one prolonged transfiguration. In those few, brief moments He did reveal the glory which was really His, but at all other times He appealed through the humanity which was like unto ours. His fatigue at Jacob's well, His tears over Jerusalem, His agony in the garden, His sufferings on the cross—all the "weakness" of His human nature—have won more souls to Him than the blazing garments and the Heavenly Voice of Thabor.

In like manner, if the life of the Church had been one triumphant, blazing transfiguration on a mountain top, apart from the woes and ills of man, she would never have been the Comforter of the Afflicted and the Refuge of Sinners. She has been called, like her divine Head, to be a redemptress, lifting men from the shadows of sin to the tabernacles of grace where saints are made.

She is not a far-off, abstract ideal, but a Mother; and though she has been stained with dust in her long journey through the centuries, though some of her children have left her and saddened her soul, yet there is joy in her heart because of the children she has nourished; there is gladness in her eyes because of the faith she has preserved; there is understanding in her soul for she has known the frailty of our flesh, and how to nourish us back to life. And in these qualities one divines the reason why our blessed Lord chose, not a sinless man like John, but a weak, frail, fallen man like Peter as His first vicar, in order that, through his weakness, he and the Church of which he is the head might sympathize with the weakness of his brethren, be their Apostle of Mercy and, in the truest sense of the term, the Vicar of the Savior and Redeemer of the world who came not to save the just, but the sinner.

THE INFALLIBILITY
OF THE CHURCH

DELIVERED ON FEBRUARY 3, 1935

OUR blessed Lord exercised a triple role on earth: He is teacher, He is king, and He is priest. This triple office He exercises in the Church as its Head, for through it He teaches, He governs, and He sanctifies. Today we are interested in Christ the Teacher; or, the infallibility of the Church.

To understand just how the infallible Church prolongs the teaching office of Christ, it must be borne in mind that Christ is God. Being God as well as man He has the Wisdom of God. From all eternity as the divine Word He is the Thought of the Godhead, the abyss of knowledge which includes all that is known or can be known. The world itself was created by the power of that Word; human intelligence is a feeble reflection of His own; the sciences and arts, inventions and discoveries, are just so many echoes of the eternal Word who is the Wisdom of God. Then at a time preordained by God He became man, appearing in the form of a Babe and growing to His full stature as man. His coming into the world was not like that of a sightseer to a strange city, but rather like that of an artist visiting his own studio, or an author paging the books he himself has written, for in becoming incarnate the divine Word was tabernacling Himself in His own creation. His human nature in no way limited His divine wisdom, but it did give Him a new way of communicating it to men, and one quite conformable to their own nature. Through a human tongue like their own, speaking their own dialect, men heard Him say, "I am the light of the world"; they saw His lips move, and for the first time in the history of the world they heard one equate Himself with Truth saying to Pilate: "I am come to give testimony of the truth."

Now it is quite unthinkable that all this wisdom should be lost, for it is the truth of God Himself. It is even unthinkable that He who was so emphatic about every "iota" of His truth being accepted, and who condemned those who would not believe, and who remained three years on earth to teach its details to the tardy intellects of His time, and who died rather than surrender the truth of what He taught, should allow this same divine truth to be forgotten, to be twisted, turned, misinterpreted, interpolated, and explained away as if it were worth no more than the babble of a child. One needs only to recall how the earthly wisdom of an Aristotle was altered by his disciples to realize the need of an agency to preserve truth. It hardly seems consonant with the nature of God to allow the branches of His vine to be poisoned, or to go back on His promise that He would send the Spirit of Truth which would preserve His followers from the spectre of evil and the gates of hell.

If God in His providential ordering of the universe bestows on vegetables and plants and flowers the power of drawing up from the soil and out of the atmosphere what is good for them, and rejecting what is evil; if He has implanted in the birds and beasts an unerring instinct which enables them to ward off the forces of decay and to preserve the original endowment of life; if He gives to man the light of reason to enable him to choose what is good for his human perfection and to reject that which cannot be healthfully incorporated into his moral fiber; if God has answered the cry of hunger on the lips of a newborn babe with the chalice of nourishment in the heart of a mother; if He has met the cry of man for light with the sun to guide his steps and illumine his way—then why should He not meet the instinctive cry of our hearts that the beautiful truths of His earthly life be preserved by something higher than the instinct of an animal or the erring reason of a man or the light of a sun that sets. Should not He who is Truth itself find a way to preserve that truth as He has found a way to preserve the earth He has made, and the man He has made to rule it? I could never doubt the divinity of Christ after hearing His prophecies and learning of His miracles; there is only one thing that could make me doubt it, and that is that He should leave this earth without leaving the salt to preserve His truth. If His own life could not be taken away from Him by a crucifixion, how could we believe that His truth which is identical with that life could ever perish through the fickleness of men?

He should have left a means to preserve His truth, a channel to prolong His teaching, or an instrument to communicate His voice. The means He chose are so very natural both to His way of dealing with men and our way of learning truth, that it often escapes us because of its simplicity. The means He chose to prolong His teaching are the same as those He chose to communicate it originally, namely, through a body with a head and living voice.

It was through a body assumed from the womb of the Virgin Mary, overshadowed by the Holy Ghost, that He communicated to us His eternal truths; it is, as we have proved elsewhere, through the Mystical Body assumed from the womb of humanity, and overshadowed by the Pentecostal spirit, that He prolongs and preserves and teaches those same eternal truths. Hence to that Church we give the same obedience, and find the same peace, as we would have if we heard Christ Himself speak them in His human body and heard His words float away on the breeze by a Galilean lake. In other words, the infallibility of the Church is nothing more than the infallibility of Christ. If Christ is God, and therefore infallible, then the Church which He founded under a visible head and infused with His Spirit, must necessarily be infallible. Infallibility is nothing more or less than the gift of Christ's Spirit to His Mystical Body which enables it to speak the mind of Christ. The infallibility of the Vicar of Christ, the head of that Body, is merely the visible expression of the invisible Head who is Christ. "He that heareth you heareth me." There is, for example, in my mind a truth: two and two are four. That truth has no weight, no color, no latitude, no longitude; it is real, but invisible. Now suppose I write it out in symbols on a piece of paper, or speak it so that others may hear it. In that case it becomes visible or objective or concrete, but it does not become a *new truth*. The truth in my mind and the truth on the paper and on my tongue are one and the same. The only difference is that in the latter case, I objectivated or articulated what was previously invisible and spiritual. This rather imperfect analogy does afford some hint of the relation of Christ the invisible Head of the Mystical Body, to Peter the visible Head. When the Vicar of Christ, the successor of Peter, proclaims an infallible truth he does not make an absolutely new and personal pronouncement; he merely articulates and objectivates the mind of Christ. He enunciates no new truth apart from Christ, he merely makes visible the invisible truth of Christ. The Church is infallible because Christ is infallible—there is no escape except to say that Christ is not Truth, that He did not prolong it, did not guarantee its preservation, and did not mean what He said when He promised to keep the Church from error until the end of days. But to say that is to surrender even the hope of living.

FULTON J. SHEEN

The dominant note of the modern world is confusion. It has not only lost its way; it has even thrown away the map. It stands bewildered, lost, stunned, afraid to enthuse or even trust lest its new love prove as unfaithful and as fickle as the others. Some solace for its bewilderment it finds by repeating: "We must just go on experimenting, for we know not where we are going, or why we are here." But it is only for a moment. Each *con* has its *pro*, each *pro* its *con*; every lunatic has his "case," every fool admits "another side," and every sphinx a thousand answers to every ten questions. When brought face to face with the certitude a Catholic has in his faith, or the peace of soul and security and the feeling of "being at home" a convert has in coming into the Church, the confused modern attributes it to excessive credulity, to the surrender of reason, to priest-craft—in a word to anything and everything except the real reason, namely, the discovery of truth.

What are we asking for in the world today? The bankers' money? The power of kings? The plaudits of the mob? None of these things do we seek. What we are asking for, if we are honest with ourselves, is certainty—a tiny atom of unquestionable divine truth. We cannot live without it; we scan every eye, knock at every door, watch every lip, and fathom a thousand hearts, to catch but a ray of certainty and truth. Who among you have listened to the Babel of confusing voices, who have read the oldest and latest wranglings of prophets, who have turned an ear to inner voices, have found that truth that strikes you prostrate on the earth like a flash of divine lightning? Truth is what you seek—a belief that cannot be shaken; a knowledge that cannot be debated; a truth that lays hold so firmly on the mind that to conceive its opposite is impossible; a truth that is the last and most solid prop of reality—a truth even that is worth dying for!

And where is that truth? That truth came to this earth nineteen hundred years ago and spoke through a physical body like unto our own. That truth is now living on earth today and speaking in a new body, the Church. Whenever then the Head of the Mystical Body, the Holy Father, teaches, I believe that Christ teaches; when the Holy Father canonizes, I believe Christ canonizes; when the Holy Father condemns an error, I believe Christ condemns an error; when the Holy Father says this is true, I believe that Christ says this is true. "He that heareth you heareth me," said our Lord. Hence my obedience to the commands of the Holy Father, because Christ is speaking through him. That is why there is on the part of the Holy Father no complacent re-echoing of the inanities of the hour, no revision of eternal truths to suit the new astrophysics, or no compromising with morals to suit immoral ways of living, no attempt to please the world, to win its favor; but there is an unmistakable effort to salt the earth, to save its soul, and to lead it unto God.

Some there are who hate Truth and nail Him to a cross; some there are who half-believe in Truth like Pilate, who turn their backs upon Him; some there are who love Truth like Peter and die like the Master died. And from that day to this—it is divine truth that makes the difference. It is divine truth that makes the Church the stumbling-block of the sceptics, the scandal of the half-hearted, the reproach of the ignorant. But no one escapes her, for they realize she stands on the crossroads of a drab civilization as the only rock of security and truth. Outside her, millions view her: some hate, some hesitate, some meditate. She gets in some people's hair; she gets in other people's brains— but she gets in *our hearts*.

THE GOVERNMENT
OF THE CHURCH

DELIVERED ON FEBRUARY 10, 1935

OUR blessed Lord is not only the teacher of God's truth and therefore infallible—He is also a King. While living in His physical body He exercised His power through the touch of a finger, the motion of His hand, the sound of His voice, all of which were the instruments of His Person, which is the Person of God. Now He lives in His Mystical Body, His power and authority remaining the same; the only difference is that now He manifests His power through human natures such as the Apostles and those who have succeeded them even to our day, namely, the bishops of the Church. They are to Christ in His glory just what His physical Body was to Him during His earthly pilgrimage. In those days the power of God rang out in a voice to the storming sea: "Be calm." In our day that same power rings out in the voice of a successor of the Apostles—the power behind the voice remaining always the same. Why should it not be so?

If the kingship of Christ could be hidden in the form of a helpless babe, why can it not be equally hidden in the form of a Peter, a James, a John, or a bishop who is their successor?

If God can communicate His power to a human nature made one with His divine Person in the Incarnation, why can He not continue to communicate it through other human natures made one with Him by the unifying spirit of Pentecost? If God has chosen to reveal His invisible divinity through a visible body, why should he suddenly stop that condescension? Once that human nature was glorified in Heaven, why should He not continue to manifest Himself through other human natures made one by His Spirit of Truth? His Mystical Body, the Church, is therefore the very thing we should expect of the goodness of God, for it is modelled upon the plan of the Incarnation. It, too, is a union of the divine and the human, the visible and the invisible, the spiritual and the material.

If I am scandalized at the thought that Christ gives His power to the Apostles and their successors, why should I not be more scandalized that the power of God once manifested itself in a human nature that could be nailed to a cross? If I am scandalized that the bishops of the Mystical Body exercise power in name, then why should I not be scandalized that the power of God should teach the doctors of the law in the form of a child only twelve years of age? How else could this power and authority be preserved except by communicating it to a new body which would preserve it because filled with His Holy Spirit? A book could not preserve His authority, for the book needs interpretation, and who would interpret it? There has never been a society without a government, a family without a head, a nation without a ruler, or a body without a brain; and in each instance the authority is vested not in a code or a constitution but in a person who safeguards and applies and judges it. Only a living body united with Christ as branches and vine can meet the demands of living men and women. And there is no more reason for doubting the authority of bishops of that body, to whom the fullness of His power was communicated, than there is for doubting that the voice of Christ, who once spoke a crude Galilean dialect to His fishermen, was in very truth the voice of God.

The following example will help us understand how Christ in Heaven exercises His power through His Mystical Body. The soul through the brain is the source whence radiates the directions, the commands to the hands and feet and other members of my body. I will, for example, to move my hand. That resolution is invisible; it has no color, no weight, no latitude, or longitude. In other words it is spiritual. But that invisible resolution is communicated through my brain and through my nerves until it finally becomes visible in the lifting of my hand. Now in the Church something like this takes place. Just as the lifting of my hand is only the visible expression of an invisible command, so too the authority of the Apostles and bishops in the Church is only the visible manifestation of the invisible power or authority which is Christ.

The authority of the bishops then is not theirs; it is His who chose them and sent them, just as the resolution belongs not to my visible hand but to my invisible will. When the Holy Father teaches, Christ teaches; when the bishops govern, it is Christ the King who rules. When the bishops of the Church in union with Peter give commands to the universal Church, and when the bishop in his diocese gives commands to his particular churches, their authority is for us in the truest sense of the word the very authority of Christ. We would think it just as serious to disobey their legitimate authority in the Mystical Body as it would be for us to disobey Christ if we saw Him in His physical Body along the shores of Galilee. They are the very voice of Christ ringing through His Mystical Body, the kingly branches of Him, the King-Vine, the Apostles of Him who is Apostolicity, the shepherds of Him who is the Shepherd of all—and whatsoever they bind on earth shall be bound also in heaven, and whatsoever they loose on earth shall be loosed also in heaven. If we deny this, then we shall have to deny Christ, who certainly meant what He said to His Apostles in saying: "My powers I give unto you… And behold I am with you all days even to the consummation of the world."

There are two great characteristics of the Church's authority: It is *impersonal* and it is divine. The authority of the Church is impersonal. That is, the lawfully constituted apostolic body does not possess authority in its own name, but only because it is representative of Christ Himself. It is therefore a great error to say: "I do not want a Church, or a pontiff, or a bishop, to stand between Christ and me." The Church does not stand between Christ and men any more than the Supreme Court, the Congress, and the President, stand between the authority of the United States and me. The Church is Christ—the total, permanent Christ of the centuries. The human instruments of Christ the King are therefore to be judged not by themselves, but by Him who sent them in His name, just as the general is to be judged not by the tone of his voice but by his right to command. "He that heareth you, heareth me," said our Lord. These words imply that He, Christ the King, would govern through others, and that those who accepted the commands of those whom He sent would be obeying Him. The commands are the words of human natures, but the authority is the authority of God.

When, therefore, the episcopacy under the headship of Peter binds and looses, rules and governs, we always look to the Person of Christ behind it, just as when we hear a voice on the radio we always look for its source, not in the machine which communicates it, but in the living person who sends it forth on the invisible waves of ether. It may happen that the human failings of one exercising authority make it difficult to envisage Christ speaking through him, but that should not make us doubt that Christ speaks, any more than static on our own radio makes us doubt the clear tones of the one who speaks from the studio.

Their authority is impersonal; they are only the instruments and representatives, and even in the strongest of their commands the words of our Lord ring forever: "One is your master—Christ."

The second characteristic note of the authority of the Church is that it is divine. This follows from the fact that those who exercise authority are merely the representatives of Christ; they have no rights over the kingship of Christ and cannot alter His laws.

Human institutions may change their creeds and beliefs because they are man-made. But the truths of the Church are God-made, and hence man may not unmake them. The Church is merely the trustee of the talents and when her Bridegroom cometh, she must not only return to Him the original deposit of truth, but she must also show an interest on them in the increased harvest of those who have faith in His Word. Her jealousy of truth is merely the love of the Master for the truth for which He died rather than compromise it. Heaven and earth might pass away but His Word would not pass away.

It may seem harsh to the outside world that Christ and His Church should be so intolerant of error, but that is not because the Church is narrow; it is only because she is a lover of truth. A heresy is like a poison in an organ of the human body, endangering the life of the organism. Just as the human body must sometimes submit to the amputation of a diseased member in order to preserve the life of the body, so too the Church must occasionally amputate some of the erring members of the Mystical Body who refuse to accept divine truth—because they endanger the health of the Body of Christ—and that amputation is called excommunication. If we thought just as much of eternal truth as we do of human life, we would think heresy just as serious as disease; and if we loved eternal truth more than human life— and we should—then we would think excommunication more necessary than amputation. The body is worth more than the raiment, the soul is worth more than the body. But though the heresy is condemned it does not follow that the heretic is lost. Due reparation made, the Church will always accept a heretic back into the treasury of her souls, but never the heresy into the treasury of her wisdom.

Obedience to these divine commands no more destroys my freedom than the laws of grammar restrict my speech, or the road restricts my travel. The laws of the Church are limitations imposed on us by Christ, it is true, but, obedience to them is the gateway to freedom. Just as I am free to draw a triangle only on condition that I obey its intrinsic law and give it three sides, so too I am free to be a Christian only on condition that I obey the laws of Christ in the Church. The Church does not dam up the river of thought; she builds levees to prevent it from overflowing and ruining the countryside. She does not build great walls around rocky islands in the sea in order to prevent her children from playing; she builds them to prevent her children from falling into the sea and thus making all play impossible. The more I obey the laws of Christ in His Church the freer I become. This is precisely what our Lord meant when He said: "The truth will make you free."

Such is the liberty of the children of God; such is the freedom we the cells of the Mystical Body enjoy. We obey only what Christ wills through the representatives of His Body, we think only what He thinks in the ambassadors of His Body, and we love only what He loves through the shepherds of His Body. We are enslaved, if you will, but only at one point: we are slaves to the Kingship of Christ, but that one point is like the fixed point of a pendulum and from it we swing in beautiful rhythm with the freedom of Him who can do all things, and therefore can make us free from everything, except the joy of having eternal bliss. Consciousness that He, the Truth, speaks through His Church, alone accounts for that beautiful childlike spirit and simple obedience which we render as sheep to the shepherds of His flock. That is why there wells up from our hearts and bursts on our lips the cry of joyful acceptance. "Speak, Lord, for thy servant heareth." Speak, Lord, for thy truth makes us free from error; speak Lord, for we hear thee, through Peter; speak, Lord, for thou hast a voice on earth in thy white shepherd of the Vatican; speak, Lord, for now we see that the root of all the liberties of the Church is the most glorious liberty of all—the freedom to become a saint.

* * *

THE PRIESTHOOD
OF THE CHURCH

DELIVERED ON FEBRUARY 17, 1935

IN the natural order there is no such thing as spontaneous generation: the mere combination of physical and chemical elements does not produce life. Life can come only from life. What is true in the natural order is true also in the supernatural order: divine life does not come from human life, any more than human life comes from a chemical. There is no such thing as a man being kind and generous in the human order, and then by increase of these purely natural virtues suddenly becoming a child of God in the supernatural order. Divine life is not an urge from the dust; it is a gift from heaven.

That gift from heaven walked this earth in the person of our blessed Lord. Until then men knew divine life only in its broken fragments; now they saw that life in Christ the Priest, who through the instrumentality of a human nature forgave sins, blessed, commanded Apostles to baptize, saved souls that were lost, and above all gave His Life for the redemption of many.

But after His Ascension into Heaven, how did this Fountainhead of divine life communicate that life to man? He communicated it in the same way He communicated His truth and His power, namely, through His Mystical Body, the Church. Since He had chosen a human nature as the instrument for the sanctification of men during His historical life, so would He use a corporation of human natures as the instrument for the sanctification of men until the end of time. Just as the invisible energy of my brain descends into all parts of my body, giving movements to arms and legs, muscles and sinews, so there descend beams of glory from the glorified Christ to the members of His Mystical Body. He even went so far as to determine the precise manner in which He would sanctify souls in His Mystical Body, the Church; namely, through the Sacraments.

What is a sacrament? In the broad sense a sacrament is a material, visible thing used as a channel for the spiritual and the invisible. The world is made up of sacraments of the natural order. A handshake is a sacrament, in the sense that it is a visible clasping of hands to express the invisible; namely, welcome and friendship. A kiss is a kind of sacrament, for it too is a visible expression of something invisible and spiritual, namely, love.

If then the universe is a kind of sacrament, because through its matter spiritual things are signified, as a flag is a symbol of a country; and if man himself is a kind of sacrament, because made up of a body through which the soul reveals itself; and if our Lord Himself is a sacrament because through His flesh, He communicated to us the Life of the invisible God, why should not He, after His Ascension, make the sacramental principle universal, and use material things as the channels for the communication of His divine life? If we were just spirits like angels, then it would not be necessary for Him to use a visible sign for His divine life; but being a compound of both matter and spirit, sacraments are necessary. Otherwise how would we know when we received invisible divine life?

Was it not fitting then that our Lord not only chose men out of His Mystical Body to be the ministers giving His life to men, but also that He chose bread, wine, oil, water, from the material universe and led them back to union with Him by making them the signs of His invisible grace? Why should not Christ the priest be the priest not only of hearts, but also of the material things which once pulled hearts away from Him? Why should not Calvary have its repercussion on the material universe as well as Eden? Why should not He, the divine Pharmacist who made minerals, roots, and vegetables, as medicine for the natural life of men, also make use of the corn and the grape and the oil as the medicine for His supernatural life. Why, in a word, should not He, the Head of the Mystical Body, lift up the crude matter of the visible world to become the dignified signs of His invisible life poured into our hearts in order that we might become in the language of St. Peter, "partakers of the divine nature"? Thus would all things once more serve God through men, and sing with the three youths in the fiery furnace a living *Benedicite* to God the Creator. Such is the wisdom of God in instituting Sacraments; the visible signs of the invisible grace by which our Lord and Savior Jesus Christ vivifies the members of His Mystical Body.

How many sacraments has Christ chosen to vivify His Mystical Body? Since the supernatural life is modelled upon human life we would expect the number to be seven, and such it actually is. But why seven? Because there are seven conditions upon which life is possible; five which condition our individual life, and two which condition our social life. In the individual order the first condition of all life is birth, for obviously unless I am born, I cannot live. In the supernatural order too, unless I am born to Christ, I cannot live His life—and this is the Sacrament of Baptism.

Second, in the natural order a man must not only be born; but he must also grow from infancy to maturity. In the supernatural order a soul too must grow to spiritual maturity as a perfect cell in the Mystical Body, so that it may overcome obstacles against that divine life—and this is the Sacrament of Confirmation.

Third, in order to live naturally a life must nourish itself. In the supernatural order a soul must nourish the divine life already within it—and this is the Eucharist.

Fourthly, in the natural order it sometimes happens that a part of the body may become injured in which case the wound must be bound and healed. In the supernatural order, it may sometimes happen that a soul may sin, in which instances a member of the Mystical Body becomes wounded, or even dies. The spiritual wound must be healed and the inanimate member revivified—and the sacrament which restores it to the life of Christ after sin is the Sacrament of Penance.

Fifthly, the last condition of life in the natural order is the driving out of the effects of disease; for a body may not only be wounded, it may suffer from the physical weakness which follows a disease. In the supernatural order the soul must be freed from the remains of sin, or the moral weakness which comes in the wake of sin—and this is the Sacrament of Extreme Unction.

Now to pass to the two other conditions of life which affect us as social beings—for we are not only individuals but also members of society.

In the natural order society is conditioned upon the procreation of our species. In the supernatural order the growth of the Mystical Body is conditioned upon the raising up of children of God—and this is the Sacrament of Matrimony.

Finally, as a social being man must also be governed. This implies officials whose business it is to apply the fruits of law and order to their neighbors. In the supernatural order, too, the members of the Mystical Body must also be governed, and this implies ministers in order that the effects of the Redemption may be applied to souls—and such is the Sacrament of Holy Orders, or the Priesthood.

The seven Sacraments are thus channels by which Christ in Heaven builds up His Mystical Body on earth by the infusion of His divine life. They are the bridges between Christians and Christ in His glory; the veins of the Mystical Body carrying the Blood of redemption from the Sacred Heart to the members of that Body; the channels through which the waters of everlasting life pour forth into the garden of the soul. The Sacraments are the kisses of God under the visible sign of which He floods the soul with the riches of His love.

Do not say: "What effect can a little water have which is poured on the head of a child?" Judge not the existence of those divine outpourings by the matter you see in the sacraments which are but the sign of the life within; judge not Baptism by the water, or the Eucharist by the bread, any more than you judge the joy of friendship by a handshake or an embrace. What is the spoken word but the air put in movement? But when the soul is in it, it becomes eloquence, justice, truth, courage to do and die! Think then of what a word is when God puts His soul into it! What is water but a union of hydrogen and oxygen? Put the genius of man into it and it becomes vapor, commerce, power, civilization. Think then what water is when God puts Himself into it! What is bread but the mere chemical combinations of wheat, water, and yeast? Unite it with the soul of man and it becomes strength, life, food, joy. Think then of what bread is when God unites His life with it. And so on for the other sacraments; that which strikes the eye in them is weak and poor, but that which strikes the soul in them is divine.

A short time ago I said that what the world was seeking without knowing it is the truth of Christ continued in the infallibility of the Church. Now I add that this same world, without knowing it, is really seeking the life of Christ the Priest in the

Sacraments of the Church. We all know the life of the body is the soul, but how many of us know that the life of the soul is Christ? Just as a body without a soul is dead, so a soul without the life of Christ is dead.

No vague theories about life, no humanitarian service, no natural fellowship, can really fill the emptiness of a soul made for the very life of God. Only the sun and rain can slake the thirst of the flower, only food and drink can satisfy the body of man, only the soul can give life to the body, and only God can give life to the soul. When therefore Christ communicates His divine life to the members of His Mystical Body in the Sacraments, He is like a mother drawing her babe to her breast, give unto us the very substance of His life. Unless He gives it, how shall we possess it? Unless He bestows it, how shall we thrill with it? How can the moisture in the earth thrill to life, unless the roots come down to it and take it unto itself; how can plants share in the sentiency of animals, unless the animals assimilate them as food; how can birds and beasts share in our thinking and willing, unless we draw them into our human life? In like manner how can we human beings thrill with divine life, unless that divine life comes down to us? And the ordinary channels God has chosen to let loose upon our souls the torrents of His divine life are the Sacraments of the Church.

The procession of life then is not upwards from the beast to man, but downwards from God to man. The source of divine life whence the great procession starts is in the Godhead: Father, Son, and Holy Ghost. From out that immensity the procession of life moved as the Father sent His divine Son into the world of broken hearts. Assuming a human nature from the Blessed Mother, the procession of divine life moved on the earth in the person of Jesus Christ, and finally wound its way up the hill called Calvary; and on a Friday called Good a soldier struck a lance into the side of that Sacred Humanity. The procession of life moved on—blood and water poured forth; blood the price of our redemption, water the symbol of our regeneration. The Son sent by His Father now returns to the Father and from the Eternal Godhead the procession of life moves on as the Father and the Son send their Holy Spirit full of truth and love to the Church on the day of Pentecost. Striking that Mystical Body, as the brightness of the sun striking a prism splits up the seven rays of the spectrum, the procession of divine life broke up into the seven Sacraments to flood the members of that Body with divine life for the seven states from the cradle to the grave. And the procession of life moves on. For nineteen hundred years it has flowed from the Head in Heaven to the Body on earth, without increase or decrease, for as creation added nothing to the being of God, so the Church added nothing to the life of God. And the procession of life moves on as Christ once more walks the earth in His Mystical Body. The river Jordan flows into every Baptismal font as Christ baptizes a soul into His Mystical Body. The Pentecost fires blaze again at every confirmation as Christ sends His Spirit to make us valiant soldiers of His Body on earth. The Cenacle table is moved to our communion-rails as Christ once more gives the Bread of Life that the members of His Body may be as one as He and the Father are one. Simon's house, where Magdalen entered, is become a confessional box as Christ once more raises His hand to penitent sinners bidding them go in peace and sin no more. The cross of the penitent thief at the right of Calvary's central cross becomes the symbol of a million deathbeds as Christ once more purifies the soul for its last journey into Paradise even on the very day of death. Cana's nuptials are repeated at the foot of every altar as Christ once more blesses the love which unites man and wife in an unbreakable bond, as the Holy Spirit has united Him and His Spouse, the Church, in union of bliss through the endless eternity. The Last Supper is revivified at every ordination ceremony as Christ once more says to those whom He has chosen out of the world: "Do this for a commemoration of me."

And finally when the great procession of life has wound its way through all nations and all peoples infusing them with the divine life unto the fullness and perfection of His Mystical Body, then shall the Procession turn back once more to its source in Heaven, where all nature will be subject to man as in the sacramental principle, and where all men will be subject to Christ, as in the Incarnation, and where Christ in His human nature shall be subject to the Father. Then shall God be all in all in heaven, where faith shall be no more, because we shall see; where hope shall be no more because we shall possess; but where there shall be only charity—for love endureth forever.

THE CHRISTIAN LIFE

DELIVERED ON FEBRUARY 24, 1935

THE Church is the Body of Christ. This idea, taken from many passages in St. Paul, has rung like an antiphon through all the broadcasts up to this point. Now we shift the emphasis from the body to the cells which make it up, or in other words, from the Church to its members.

It is important to do this for one of the most erroneous ideas in religion today is that religion is a purely individual relationship between the soul and God. How often we hear it said: "I can worship God better by myself than with others." This is equivalent to saying: "I can serve America better by myself than with others." It forgets that man is a social being and that his relation to God is in some way a relation to his neighbors. The divine law of love embraces both: Love God and love your neighbor. The spiritual life therefore, in addition to the enrichment of our personal life, also commits us to the social life of the Kingdom of God. Hence in the greatest of all Christian prayers taught by our Lord Himself, we do not say: "My Father who art in Heaven," nor do we say: "Give me this day my daily bread"—which we would say if religion were a private relation between God and the soul. Rather were we told to say: "*Our* Father who art in heaven"—"Give *us* this day *our* daily bread." The very words "Thy kingdom come" imply that we as individuals are incorporated into a supernatural society, that we are, in a word, members of the Church, the Mystical Body of Christ.

It may strike us as strange that God should make the normal growth of our spiritual self depend upon our membership in His Mystical Body or His kingdom on earth; but once we look over the natural order we see that such is the law of all life. Is not every living thing in the universe in some way conditioned by its environment? Does not each individual life live in a kingdom? The fish, for example, can live only in the environment of water; the plants live by communion with the sunlight and moisture; the cells live through their membership with other cells in the kingdom of the body; the bee lives in the hive, the child in the family, and the citizen in the nation. Now the supernatural order is built upon the order of nature.

Hence the Christian is a part of a whole, a citizen of the kingdom of God, a child in the family of the Trinity, a cell in the organism of the whole Christ and a member of the Mystical Body. As St. Paul tells us: "You are the body of Christ, and members of member," for it is the "one and the same Spirit [working and] dividing to everyone according as he will…for the edifying [building up] of the body of Christ unto a perfect man, unto the measure of the age of the fullness of Christ."

The Church does not stand between Christ and me any more than the nation stands between me and patriotism. It is just as natural for my soul to live in the Church as it is for my eye to live in the environment of beauty, my lungs to live in the environment of air. The great broad world of nature does not cramp my intellect, but enlarges it by giving it an opportunity to study the secrets of nature, to tame its forces, and to harness its energies. And the great broad world of supernature, the Church, does not cabin, crib, and confine my spiritual life; it gives it an opportunity to expand its faith by belief in a larger whole, and to enlarge its charity by kindness to the other cells of that body.

The Church is the native air of the soul in the state of grace, the blood of the heart in love with God, the common ground where Christians meet in Christ, the altar where individuals forming part of the world-life of Christ kneel to say in common: "Our Father."

When therefore I am asked what the Church means to me, I answer that it is the temple of life in which I am a living stone; it is the tree of eternal fruit of which I am a branch; it is the Mystical Body of Christ on earth of which I am a member. The Church is therefore more to me than I am to myself; her life is more abundant than mine, for I live by union with her. She could live without me for I am only a cell in her body; but I could not normally live without her. I live only as a part of her, as my arm lives only as a part of my body. So absorbing does she become that her thoughts are my thoughts; her loves are my loves; her ideals are my ideals. I consider sharing her life the greatest gift God has ever given to me, as I should consider losing her life the greatest evil that could befall me. Dependence is the very essence of my creaturely existence, for no man is sufficient unto himself. I am not a speck in a moral void, nor a wanderer without a home, nor an isolated unit in creation; rather am I dependent on the God-appointed destiny whereby I *share* my love of God with others who love God in the unity of the Mystical Body of Christ. In that Body which is the fullness of Christ do I find the spiritual environment for my spiritual life; in her I live and move and have my being; from out her seven fountains I draw the waters of everlasting life; from out her Book of the Seven Seals I learn the secrets of the Lamb; from out her tabernacles I draw the Bread of Life and the wine that germinates virgins. My life is her life; my being is her being; she has my love, my service, as I myself have the entire devotion and service of my hand. She is the living organism, I am but an organ; she is the body, I am but a member; she is Life, I am the living thing; she is the Spouse of Christ, I am but a feature; she the Vine, and I the branch. "Abide in me, and I in you. As the branch cannot bear fruit of itself, unless it abide in the vine, so neither can you, unless you abide in me. I am the vine and you the branches: he that abideth in me, and I in him, the same beareth much fruit: for without me you can do nothing."

We must not think, because the fullness of our spiritual life is in the Church, that she absorbs us and leaves no room for our individual development. Just as in the natural order the individual cell has its own growth even though it dwells in the body, so in like manner the individual Christian has his own personal development even though a member of the Mystical Body. There is only one sun to shine upon all the flowers of the world, and hence all flowers are members of the kingdom of the sun. But their mutual dependence on the sun does not prevent the sun from drawing out of each flower its own particular beauty, and its own peculiar perfume. So does Christ in His dwelling in the Church give life and beauty to all who receive Him, yet to each individual soul the Mystical Body gives its special life and beauty; so much so, that there is consummated under the bowers of the Church the union of the soul and its divine Beloved which death does not part but seals in everlasting bliss.

The body is made up of many members and countless cells; each with its own personality, though all draw upon a common life and are animated by a common soul. The eye does not lose its power of vision, nor does the ear lose its sense of hearing, because they are part of the body. Neither does the soul who has a natural bent for an active life, nor the soul who has a natural bent for contemplation, lose his personality when united to the Body of Christ—for the Church still has its Marthas and its Marys. As a matter of fact, there is no legitimate natural twist or bent or leaning of any personality in the world, that cannot find its outlet in the organism of the Church. The vast multitude of religious communities in the Church give free expression to the most varied personal inclinations. A Francis who loves the poor may become a Franciscan; a Clare who loves the needy may become a Poor Clare; a Teresa who loves penance may become a Carmelite; a Dominic who loves study and preaching may become a Dominican; an Ignatius who loves spiritual action may become a Jesuit; a Paul who loves the Passion of Christ may become a Passionist; a Paul who loves preaching the Gospel may become a Paulist; a Vincent who loves the orphans may become a Vincentian; and so on for the hundreds of communities within the Church. Yet in each of these communities itself each individual still has his personal devotion to his Lord and Master.

While living His historical life our Blessed Lord did not destroy the personalities of His twelve Apostles because they were one with Him, nor did He destroy the passion of a Magdalene after her conversion. He merely changed the direction of their inclinations, making them flow upward instead of downward, transforming an impetuous Simon to a daring Peter, a hating Saul into a loving Paul, a flesh-loving Magdalene into a spirit-loving Mary. Now that He has ascended into Heaven and sent His Spirit into His Mystical Body the Church, He continues to draw all souls into the common life of that body without destroying their property as a member or a cell of that body. The simple little girl of Lisieux did not cease to be a Little Flower because she became a Carmelite in the Mystical Body of Christ. Ignatius was a soldier both before and after he became the founder of the Jesuits; Louis IX was a king even though he was a subject of the King of kings; and, in like manner each and every one of us may continue to live our distinctly different lives in the office, in the field, at the machine, and at the university, in the humble duties of a routine world and in the lofty position as leaders of men, just as Thomas à Becket could wear the purple on the outside to please his people and the penitential chain on the inside to please himself.

There is no destruction of nature by grace, but only its elevation to another order. Tears are a common fountain for joy and sorrow. Passions too are common outlets for virtue and vice. It is not a different passion that makes a man a saint, from that which makes a man a devil; it is the same passion going in a different direction. The Church then in embracing our lives within her common life does not destroy our personalities—she does not even destroy our most wicked passions. She transmutes them by the magic of her Sacraments, provides new outlets, fixes new goals, and digs new channels. The heroes of the world are not different from martyrs; the same natural courage which would make a man die for Caesar on a battlefield, the Church would transmute into a supernatural courage which would make him die for Christ. The bigots are all potential missionaries, for the same zeal that makes them unwittingly serve falsehood can be elevated by the Church to make them serve divine truth. The great scientists are all incipient theologians for that same curiosity, which drives them to a knowledge of secondary causes, the Church transmutes by leading them to a knowledge of the First Cause which is God. We would not say that the hero who became a saint, nor the bigot who became a missionary, nor the scientist who became a theologian, lost their personalities once incorporated into Christ's body, any more than we lost our personalities once we became citizens of a nation. But we would say, that in their union with that common life of grace, they had found the sublimation of their distinct personalities, and the crown of their individual selves. They would see as we see, that Christ's Mystical Body is like a garden beautiful, formed by the blossoming of individual flowers each in its own beauty, but in its varied beauty blending into one harmonious rapturous delight. Each flower of that garden has its own beauty revealed as in no other flower, yet does each flower grow in beauty by contrast and by blending with the other flowers all rooted in a common soil and lighted by a common sun.

So is it in the mystical life in which Christ dwells in His Church, revealing Himself anew in each individual soul, and never in two wholly alike, here manifesting Himself in a Peter, there in a Paul, here in a Martha, there in a Mary, here in a lover of His infancy, there in a lover of His cross, here in a rose with thorns, there in a flower without them, and yet all growing more beautiful by their fellowship with other saintly flowers because all rooted in the same Christ's life and all lighted by the same Christ-truth unto the effusion of the sweet odor of sanctity sent up to the very heaven where as children of God they await the fulfillment of the prayer their own Lord made the night He went into His garden: "that they all may be one, as thou, Father, in me, and I in thee; that they also may be one in us."

ZEAL FOR SOULS

DELIVERED ON MARCH 3, 1935

THE great characteristic of life is growth. Youth and growth are synonymous; age and decay are synonymous. Life has therefore been properly defined as the sum of those forces which resist death. The law of growth was imposed on creation when God told man and the lower creatures of which He was the Master: "Increase and multiply." The same law of growth was imposed on supernature, or the Church, when our Lord told His Apostles: "Preach the gospel to every creature." The Church was thus ordered to reproduce, to generate new life, to fill up the Kingdom of God, to make conquests from the outside, to increase progeny from within; for the Church that does not reproduce, that is not missionary, is weaving its own shroud. "You have not chosen me," said our Lord, "but I have chosen you; and have appointed you, that you should go, and should bring forth fruit, and your fruit should remain."

But just how is this Mystical Body of Christ to grow from a mustard seed into a great tree? Is it to grow by God pouring out His grace on the souls of men, while we the members remain inactive? Or is it to grow by members co-operating with the grace of God? The laws of nature suggest the answer. The human body develops from infancy to perfection, thanks principally to food and drink. But food and drink would not make the body grow unless the body already possessed a soul which is the principle of life. Corpses do not grow regardless of how much nourishment is poured into them.

Neither does the soul alone suffice for life. The food which the living body needs comes to the body through the members of the body; the feet which walk to the table and the hands which touch it and take it into the organism. Thus two factors combine for growth: the living soul, and food given to the body through the help of the body itself.

The Church is the Mystical Body of Christ. Its soul is the Spirit of Christ, without which the Church would not be an organism, but only an organization. Its body is made up of all who have been incorporated unto Christ by Baptism. But the body and soul alone are not enough to account for the growth of the Church. The growth of the Church like the growth of the human body, depends for its development on the activity of its members. The fact that we share the life of Christ does not dispense us from the obligation of working with Him for the increase of His Mystical Body. Do not the branches reach out to absorb the sunlight; do not the hands and feet reach out to grasp the food? Why then should not our Lord, in like manner, make the growth of His Church dependent upon its members? He might have done otherwise. But since Mary was called to share in the Redemption, since Apostles were called to preach what Christ had preached, since Peter was called to be the rock of His Church, aye, since the call of Abraham and the endowing of Adam with free will, it is by means of men that God deals with men. As the diamond is polished only by the diamond, so it is by and through human natures that Christ spreads the Kingdom of His Father. The zealous souls, the Apostles, the missionaries in far countries, the saintly souls in our own land, the sisters in our schools, the priests in our parishes, all the Christ-loving men and women whose hearts are on fire with the love of God, are the eyes, the feet, and the hands of Christ which reach out to the pagan, the dejected, the forlorn, the humanists, the sinners, the erring, to lift them into the Body where they may be quickened again into life and love and truth by the vivifying power of the Spirit of Christ.

What nobler work could there be than zeal for souls? What finer way to spend oneself and be spent than in drawing souls to the love of their Lord and their God? The world holds in high repute the physicians who restore health to the diseased, the surgeons who amputate the cancerous growth, the teachers who bring history and grammar to the illiterate, the social workers who rehabilitate the broken human earthenware of our streets, and the scientists who extend the frontiers of our science beyond another star. All this is noble, but since there is a life beyond this, let it be remembered that in the Book of Life they are written in letters of gold who do for souls what those have done for the body. The great heart of Christ holds in eternal love those spiritual physicians who restore grace to diseased sinners, those spiritual surgeons who root out the cancer of error that truth may grow, those teachers who bring knowledge of grace to the learned, those sisters of charity who make saints out of Magdalenes, and those missionaries who extend the frontier of Christ beyond the last Christian. These are Christ's fishermen who stand by the waters of the baptismal font to catch souls for the Kingdom of God; these are Christ's shepherds who feed the lambs and the sheep with the Bread of everlasting life and the Wine that germinates virgins.

The responsibility to extend the Mystical Body of Christ devolves upon each and every one of its members. Any member who refuses the right of way to life by denying it facilities for transmission is guilty of a breach of trust. The privilege of being a cell in the Mystical Body is the privilege of a stewardship of service and of apostolate. Through loyalty to this missionary imperative each member may pay his debt of thanks for the gift of faith by endowing the future with that faith. Every living unit thus stands between the past and the future with obligations to both which it cannot default. What we have received, we must pass on and not pocket. What has been given to us must not be confined but cradled for growth. As guardians of the divine life which has come down to us since Pentecost, we must answer to God for misappropriation and impounding to our own ends. Every talent received must bear interest, and every grace received must furnish a highway along which the Gospel of Christ shall have a straight and unimpeded path for propagation.

God has implanted in nature a tremendous enthusiasm for new life. The Holy Spirit has implanted in the Church even a greater enthusiasm for new life. In the nature of things all life is aglow with the missionary spirit. Look to the trees in the spring-time. The gold and silver of their blooming is the beautiful and fragrant expression of life's loyalty to life and new life. The very efflorescence is evidence of how serious it is about its business. It is making life's supreme effort to fulfill its stewardship. Every bloom is a declaration of trust; every blossom is a deposit to be held as a trust for posterity, a cradle for the slowly forming fruit, and a token of how in the supernatural order every member of the Church Militant should sow the seed of God's truth in every soul he meets. We are commanded to love our neighbor, but there is no higher way to love him than to help him to love the common Father and the Son whom He has sent. We do not save our souls alone, but only in conjunction with others.

Occasionally missionary effort demands sacrifice. We may be called upon to offer generously for those who go as mis-sionaries, or to pray for them; but in each instance the sacrifice

will be a joy, for its inspiration will be love. If there ever came
a time when we would have to choose between preserving our
own goods or even our own physical life in order to pass on to
a future generation, as apostles, the spiritual life of the Church,
then we must make the surrender of the lower values. If there is
not sufficient vitality for life and fruit, and the tree must choose
between living its life and being disloyal to the law of repro-
duction, it will always choose to die. Horticulturists have taken
advantage of this fact in treating vines that are not doing their
best; by cutting the bark, they practically scare a dilatory vine
into believing it is about to die, and immediately it hurries and
even doubles its output in fruit. Here we see the secret of the
lavish output of blossom, bud, and fruit. It is the sacrificial principle at work. Victim and priest in one, the fruit in bloom lays
out its best upon the altar, literally pouring out its life that it
may redeem the earth from future barrenness and make solitary
places glad. And while the sacrificial act for future generations is
going on, nature puts on her beautiful garments, flooding over
with fragrance from her myriad censers amidst the stately rit-
ual of springtime and the music of singing birds. In like manner, the Church cannot be missionary, unless it is sacrificial and
happy in the sacrifice. As He who hung on the Tree of Life has
His Heart pierced by a spear only to pour forth the reproductive blood and waters of the Eucharist and Baptism, so too the
Church, a product of that sacrificial act, must in virtue of the
law of inheritance be sacrificed that the Lord's prayer may be
fulfilled and that His Kingdom may come, and the mustard seed
may grow into the Tree of Life. The deaths of the martyrs, the
priests and nuns in the foreign missions of the world, the alms of
the poor given until it hurts, the prayers of those who know the
Body must grow, are not separate and unconnected incidents

in a world of space and time. They are a necessary part of the divine plan, making their contribution to the great redeeming purpose which issues in the home-bringing of all God's wandering children to the warmth and welcome of the house not made with hands.

To all the members of the Mystical Body, then, there goes out the command to increase and multiply, to save other souls, to illumine other minds, to enkindle other hearts with the torch of love lit at the first burning on the altar of God. The gold of our prayers, the frankincense of our alms, and the myrrh of sacrifice, are the means by which we fulfill our stewardship, pouring out our reproductive power so that a day may come when India's absolute renunciation of personality will be transformed into a renunciation wherein personality is not extinguished but perfected in Christ; that a day may come when Hindu monasteries will be surmounted by the cross; when the Orient will learn from the West not only how to use our machinery, but also how to say our prayers; that schools of contemplation may be opened in thoughtful Asia where the deeds of the anchorites will be repeated in the forests ere industrial progress robs them of their lost solitude; that the islands of the Pacific may be caught in the fishermen's net and pay veneration to Peter; that heathen lands may take from us not only our electricity but also our sanctuary lamp; that the vast army of those who have lived on the fringe of Christianity and know it not, may learn of it from us, that we may vindicate our right to have and hold the possessions which we enjoy; and, finally, that black hands may one day hold up white hosts from the rising to the setting of the sun, and all the world may know how sweet is the heart of Christ.

* * *

THE SPIRIT OF CHRIST

DELIVERED ON MARCH 10, 1935

HOW often we hear souls bemoan the fact that they are so distant from Galilee, and so removed from Jesus. We hear them say that they long to have lived when He walked the earth, to have heard Him speak the Beatitudes with sweetness and authority, to have watched Him dignify common labor at the carpenter's bench, to have stood beneath the cross with Mary, and on Easter to have seen Him walk in the newness of life, and like Thomas to have put their fingers into the wounds and their hands into His side to be forever convinced He was their Lord and their God.

Others wish not so much that they lived in His day, but rather that He lived unto our own. What a joy they think it would be if He walked our earth today, if they could go to Him in their moments of doubt and be consoled by His divine peace, kneel at His feet and have him wash away the foul debt of their sin, bring their children to have Him lay His hands upon them, see Him enter the great cathedrals bearing His name, and above all else watch Him preach the doctrines of economic and social justice and heal the lame and halt as He walked down the streets of our city, as He once walked through Tyre and Sidon.

The world is full of men and women who think of our Lord solely and uniquely in terms of what their eyes can see, their ears can hear, and their hands can touch. How many there are who, starting with the truth that He was a great Teacher of commanding influence who walked the earth nineteen hundred years ago, gather up the details of the scenery of the lake and hill country of Galilee, and use their imagination better to portray the exact circumstances of His earthly life; but here the appreciation of His life ends. They have learned habitually to think of Him as someone who belongs to human history, like Caesar, Washington, or Mohammed; they think of Him as one who lived on earth and passed away. But where He is, what His nature is, whether He can act upon us now, whether He can hear us, be approached by us, are thoughts which are contemptuously dismissed as belonging to the category of theological abstractions and foolish dogmas. These very souls may follow His example in such and such an instance, apply His Beatitudes to this or that circumstance of their life, look upon His life as a great sacrifice and inspiration; but beyond that Christ means nothing to them. He is the greatest man who ever lived, but He is nothing more. They indeed are among those of whom St. Paul said that they know Christ only according to the flesh.

It must be admitted that the continued sensible and visible presence of our Savior would have been a continuous inspiration to our lives, but we must not forget that He Himself said the night before He died: "It is expedient to you that I go." Strange words, these! Why should they be spoken at a moment when He had weaned the hearts of His Apostles away from their nets, boats, and custom tables, and had entwined them so closely about His own Sacred Heart? How could it be expedient for them that He go? How could it be expedient for men who were wanderers on the sea of life that their Captain should be taken from them? How could it be expedient for them to be left alone at a moment when He was sending them out as sheep among wolves? How could it be expedient for men who lived so close to the material and the sensible to have Him whom they once had seen and touched become the great Unseen and Untouchable? And yet it was expedient for us that He go—otherwise He would not have told us so. Perhaps we can see reasons why it was expedient for Him to go.

First of all, if He had continued His earthly life to our own day, then the most important questions of life would have been left unanswered. Where does a good life lead to? What is the reward for virtue? What lies beyond the tomb? Does a saintly life purchase anything better in the next world? Has Heaven any crown for those who, like good shepherds, lay down their lives for their sheep? Certainly, if Jesus has not merited eternal glory because of His earthly life, then wherein lies the value and the worth of a good earthly life? Did not our Lord Himself tell us that "it was fitting that the Son of man should suffer in order that He might enter into His glory"? In other words, one of the reasons why it was expedient for our Lord to go was to show that the reward of a worthy life is not an earthly one, that each and every one of us has an appointed task to do in this world, that we were sent into it to work out our salvation, and that when that task is accomplished and that work done, like Him we must press onward to our "supernal vocation," which is everlasting glory with Him in Heaven.

But it was expedient for Him to go for still another reason: in order that He might be nearer to us. This is the very reason He gave for His going: "for if I go not, the Paraclete will not come to you but if I go, I will send him to you... I have yet many things to say to you: but you cannot bear them now. But when he, the Spirit of truth, is come, he will teach you all truth...he shall glorify me; because he shall receive of mine, and shall show it to you.... A little while, and now you, you shall not see me; and again a little while, and you shall see me: because I go to the

Father... I will see you again, and your heart shall rejoice; and your joy no man shall take from you."

In these solemn words spoken on the eve of His crucifixion He explicitly stated that He was going back to the boundless depths of His Father's Life whence He came, but His going would not leave them orphans, for He would come again in a new way; namely, by His Spirit. Our Lord was here equivalently saying that if He remained on earth in His physical life, He would have been only an *example to be copied*; but if He went to His Father and sent His Spirit, then He would be a *life to be lived*. If He remained visibly and tangibly with us He would have been related to us merely as a model is related to the artist who chisels his marble, but never as the idea and inspiration which produces the work of art. If He remained on earth He would have been merely the subject of prolonged observation, of scientific study and imitation; but however noble His example, however inspiring His words, He would always have been *outside us, external* to us; an *external* Voice, an *external* Life, an *external* Example—He could never be possessed other than by an embrace. The very physical body which housed that divine life would have been an obstacle to our loving Him by a unity of mind and heart and soul whence all true love must tend. If He had tarried on earth, all would have stood still. It would have been the perpetual promise of a day; a lingering blossom, a retarded fruit, a lengthening childhood, a backward maturity.

But once He ascended into heaven and sat at the right hand of the Father in the Glory which is His, then He could send His Spirit into our souls, so that He would be with us not as an external Person, but as a living Soul; then He would be not just a mere something mechanical to be copied, but a something vital to be reproduced, not a something external to be portrayed in our lives, but a something living to be developed within us. His Ascension into Heaven, and His sending of His Spirit, alone makes it possible for Him to unite Himself wholly with us, to take up His abode with us, body and blood, soul and divinity, and to be in the strictest sense of the term "Christ in us." It was expedient therefore that He go, otherwise He would have belonged to history and to a country. Now He belongs to men.

Thanks to His Invisible Spirit, which He sends into His Mystical Body, Christ is living now on earth just as really and truly as He was living in Galilee nineteen centuries ago. In a certain sense He is closer to us now than then, for His very Body then made Him external to us, but thanks to His Spirit, He can now live in us as the very Soul of our souls, the very Spirit of our spirit, the Truth of our minds, the Love of our hearts, and the Desire of our wills. Thus the life of Christ is transferred by the Spirit from the region of purely historical studies, which we investigate with our reason, to the realm of spiritual experience, where He speaks directly to our soul. It may have been a great consolation for the Canaanite woman to have touched the hem of His garment, for Magdalen to have kissed His feet, for John to have leaned on His breast the night of the Last Supper, but all these intimacies are external. They have great force and appeal because they are sensible, but none of them can even vaguely approximate the union, the intimacy, which comes by possessing Christ inwardly, thanks to His Holy Spirit. The greatest joys of life are those which come from unity—the unity of citizens in a nation, the unity of children and parents in a family, the unity of interests and ideals among friends, and the unity of two in one flesh in the Sacrament of Matrimony. But even this last kind of unity, which is the deepest in the natural order because it bears fruit in a child, is still quite imperfect. The unity of the flesh need not always mean unity of the souls. Sometimes the possession of another outwardly is the greatest obstacle to inward possession. We never reach the height of unity until there is a fusion of loves, of thoughts, and of desires, a unity so profound that we think with the one we love, love with the one we love, desire what he desires; and this unity is found in its perfection when the soul is made one with the Spirit of Christ which is the Spirit of God. The joys that come from human friendships, even the noblest, are but the shadows, and fond reflections of the joy of a soul possessed of the Spirit of Christ. Elevate human happiness, which comes from union with the one loved, to the most extreme point the heart can endure, and even that is but a spark compared to the Great Flame of the Spirit of Christ burning in a soul that loves Him.

The great tragedy of history is not that men should fall, but that they should fail to rise to full realization of their vocation as children of God, in other words that they should miss so much. All about us we see vast multitudes of men and women of refinement and culture, endowed with intelligence, possessed of every natural virtue, and every now and then swept by noble emotions and ideals, but who are living second-rate, superficial, unimportant, and morally insignificant lives, because they have never had the clay of their nature enkindled into flame by the Spirit of Christ. They may do great things for the world, they may build great bridges, harness waterfalls, accomplish great pieces of research, but they never do anything for themselves, by sounding the depths of their souls, and realizing that they can be filled only by the God that made them. The world of the supernatural has no appeal to them any more than heroism has appeal to a coward. They have become so used to the dense atmosphere of the material that they stifle in the more rarefied atmosphere of the stars that beckon to the Cenacle.

And in this lies the danger of our whole civilization which is gradually turning away from God. Nothing great, nothing really good, was ever done in this world by a human life that had not a baptism of God's Holy Spirit. There is no escape from the words of Him who presided at Creation as the Word, and at the re-creation on the cross as the Word-made flesh: "Without me you can do nothing."

In the words of St. John: "This we know that we abide in him, and he in us: because he hath given us of his spirit." Thanks to that spirit the life of Christ becomes our life in Christ. What He did in His own human nature in Galilee He is doing today in other human natures in New York, London, Paris, and in every city and hamlet of the world where there are souls vivified by His Spirit. He is still being born in other Bethlehems of the world, still coming into His own and His own receive Him not, still instructing the learned doctors of the law and answering their questions, still laboring at a carpenter's bench, still "going about doing good," still preaching, governing, sanctifying, climbing other Calvarys, and entering into the glory of His Father. There are poor people today in our bread lines, there are innocent men in our prisons, there are half-clothed families in our tenements, who are as ragged and destitute on the outside as they are rich with the Spirit of Christ on the inside. Externally they appear to most of us like the ordinary poor who attack the rich, like the common captive who harangues authority, like the selfishly needy who curse their lot, but the resemblance is only on the outside, and so many are deceived. Some eyes are so filled with the dust of the world's traffic that they cannot see the divine grace in their souls; and so the world classifies them in their social surveys as the poor, the dependent, the captive—but in the eyes of the Father in heaven they are other Christs in other deserts, thirsty at other Jacob's wells, suffering on other crosses, captive in other praetoriums. The world sees them as so many economic problems; the Heavenly Father sees them as beloved sons in whom He is well pleased.

This truth, that the Spirit of Christ dwells in the just, escapes the world. We know our Lord said it, we confess it with our lips, we believe it in our heart, but we do not seize it in all its reality. Not even the just and saintly Christians realize it as they should, and on Judgment Day even they will be surprised that Christ walked the earth again in those who were filled with His Spirit. For when He will say to them: "I was hungry, and you gave me to eat: I was thirsty, and you gave me to drink: I was a stranger, and you took me in: naked, and you covered me: sick, and you visited me: I was in prison, and you came to me," the just will "answer him, saying: Lord, when did we see thee hungry, and fed thee; thirsty, and gave thee drink? And when did we see thee a stranger, and took thee in? or naked, and covered thee? Or when did we see thee sick or in prison, and came to thee?" Then the Lord will answer and say to them: "Amen I say to you, as long as you did it to one of these my least brethren, you did it to me." What a waste! Even the social workers will have missed the glory of their vocation! They will think they fed a stomach, when lo—they broke bread for Christ and knew it not! They will think they gave a cup of water to a thirsty throat, when lo—Christ was sitting at their well! They will speak of the needy as Case No. 568 when lo—it was Christ who wore the clothes! Yes! Christ is still walking the earth in the souls of the just. The next time a soul in the state of grace asks for bread, and you respond with a bitter word and closed door, enter into your hearts and ask: "What if that man be Christ!"

THE COMMUNION OF SAINTS

DELIVERED ON MARCH 17, 1935

THE emphasis which has thus far been placed on the Mystical Body on earth might lead some to believe that it has no extension beyond the earth. It is now time to correct that impression. As the earth is bigger than any nation, as the universe is bigger than the solar system, so too the Mystical Body is bigger than the Church on earth. Did not our Lord Himself tell us that it was a supernatural society in which the members were bound together by love of a common Father? Because the Church is an organism made up of many members and yet one because possessed of the Spirit, it is possible for the members to share spiritual goods one with another, as the whole body shares the food which is taken into the stomach. The Mystical Body in its entirety includes not only its members on earth who are still working out their salvation, but those who have died in God's favor without having made payment of the last farthing of the debt of sin; and, finally, those who already have been ushered into the eternal glory and bliss. In other words, there are three great divisions of the Mystical Body of Christ: the Church militant on earth, the Church suffering in Purgatory, and the Church triumphant in Heaven. The reciprocal relation and spiritual sharing of gifts and merits between these three is what tradition has called the "Communion of Saints."

Those of us who live on earth and are incorporated to Christ actually by faith and hope and charity, but not *definitively*, constitute what is known as the Church militant. That which characterizes us is warfare, not a warfare against our brethren with the cold sword of steel, but against the powers of darkness with the warm kindly spirit of charity. We are militant in the sense that we are yet in the process of working out our salvation, exposed to the weakness of will, the surprises of temptation, the attacks of the devil, and yet constantly striving to carry our treasure of grace in a frail vessel to the judgment seat of God. The cross is to be our daily portion; the earth is a place of trial and not a lasting paradise; there are enemies to combat, and these enemies must be conquered not by crushing them but by crushing ourselves, for no one shall be crowned unless he has struggled. God hates peace in those whom He has destined for war.

The other branch of the Church is the Church suffering. Our Lord enjoined us to "work while it is day, for the night cometh when no man can work." That night, when the season of earthly merit has passed, is the moment of death. In the long course of nineteen hundred years many soldiers of the Church militant have served their allotted time and reported to their Captain Christ. Many of them served faithfully, but not too well; some of them rested on their weapons when they might have struck more heroically; others were timid for they loved with a broken and yet recovered loyalty; others, while never losing sight of their great ideal, nevertheless fell short of being perfect "as the heavenly Father is perfect." These soldiers well know they are not to be immediately ushered before the Christ with the same titles of glory as their fellow soldiers who died in the field of battle or who burned themselves out with love. Their King, therefore, in His mercy has tempered His justice and permitted them further purgation in Purgatory, where they might wash the stains from their baptismal robes, and cleanse the rust from their confirmation armor, so as to be pure and spotted enough to stand in the majestic, august presence of the all-holy God. These souls who are expiating the punishment due to their pardoned sins, form the Church suffering in Purgatory.

Finally, there is Heaven, or the Church triumphant, the place where the soldiers of earth who have fought the good fight and kept the faith and have loved God, receive the reward of eternal happiness which is their due. Every second countless members of the Church militant and the Church suffering are passing into the joys of the Church triumphant where the soul is set free to live in the depths of those things whose surface is but touched on earth: the fullness of life, of truth, and of love, which is the Father, the Son, and the Holy Ghost. There are only war veterans in heaven, who have fought the good fight for the Kingdom of God. In that glorious army of the all-conquering King are the Apostles; the white-robed body of martyrs, confessors, virgins, and pontiffs; and Holy Women, with Peter and Paul as their head—all of whom drank the Chalice of the Lord and ate the Bread of Life everlasting. There are also the angels, who had their moment of trial when Michael flashed his archangelic spears. But above the angels and above men, is that Mother of Soldiers, that Mother of Heavenly Warriors, that Mother of the Captain of all who rode forth with Him to the Battle of Calvary, and who, too, was pierced by seven swords—Mary, the Mother of Jesus, Mary, the Mother of the Mystical Body, Mary, Queen of Angels and Saints. The number of the elect is not yet complete, but as the Church on earth grows, the Mystical Body of Christ grows to its fullness until it embraces that "great multitude which no man could number, of all nations, and tribes, and peoples, and tongues, standing before the throne, and in the sight of the Lamb, clothed with white robes, and palms in their hands… saying: Benediction, and glory, and wisdom, and thanksgiving, honor, and power, and strength to our God for ever and ever. Amen."

These three divisions of the Mystical Body of Christ are not independent, but there is a constant flux and flow between them because all are filled by the same Spirit and crowned by the same Christ. The Mystical Body, like the universe, is organic and there is therefore bound to be the repercussion of merits throughout every part of it, on earth, in Heaven, and in Purgatory. If a stone is thrown into the ocean, it causes a ripple which widens in ever broadening circles until it affects even the most distant shore. A toy dropped from the cradle of an infant disturbs in some way the distant stars. This is because each part of the universe is bound up with every other part as a physical whole. In like manner each part of the Church is bound up with every other part in a more vital and intimate way, because animated by the same charity and united in a mystical whole by the Holy Spirit of God. Great vital movements flow through its members on the field of battle, on earth, or behind the lines, in Purgatory, or before the victorious King in Heaven. The first stream flows between the Church triumphant and the Church militant on earth, for the angels and saints in heaven, in answer to our prayers, can intercede for us at the throne of God. They can pour healing on our wounded wings, courage into our cowardly hearts, and the oil of strength into our weakness. They are not indifferent to our warfare, for the saints can never be indifferent to good; nor can they be indifferent to that other part of their body which we are. How could the veteran soldier at home be indifferent to the soldiers on the field of battle since both fight under the same Captain, carrying the flag of five wounds in the forefront of battle? So eager are they for victory, so keen are they for enlistments in the army of the Lamb, so zealous are they for the cause of Christ, that they lend a most attentive ear to our prayers and supplications. As our Lord intercedes to the Father for us in virtue of His merits, so do they intercede to our Lord, not through their own merits, but through His merits, the source of our sanctification.

Another great line of communication exists between the Church militant on earth and the Church suffering in Purgatory. It is indeed one of the most consoling doctrines of the faith that we can still help our loved ones after death, if they stand in need of help, and by doing so perhaps make atonement for our ingratitude to them during life. Death does not break the bond, for our fundamental unity with them is not because they shared our flesh and blood, but rather because they lived by the same Spirit and were members of the same Body under the Headship of Christ.

Now these members of the Mystical Body who died united to God in the center of their being, but not in every part of its circumference, those who died with unpaid debts, or who left the world still stained with imperfections, pass for their final purification into Purgatory, that they may be cleansed from their sins to walk the holy way of God. These poor souls suffer from one great handicap: they cannot help themselves. This is only natural, for their time of merit is passed. A soldier carried from the battlefield can no longer fight the enemy. But they can be helped by us, as the wounded soldier behind the lines may be rehabilitated by other soldiers for the great day of victory. Unless we help them they must endure the purifying purgation until the last tiny blemish of imperfection is burned away, and they are made ready "as by fire" to enter into the glory of the Church triumphant and the all-consuming love of God.

Manifold are the means by which we may help the members of the Church suffering. A loaf of bread given to the poor, a visit to a hospital to bring solace to the sick, an alms to the beggar in the street, a glass of water to a friend, a kind word in an environment of unkindness, a "Hail Mary" whispered softly as we go about our routine duties, a short indulgenced exclamation in the midst of our pleasures, a slight mortification at table—any of these, and each of these, if done out of love for God and for the intention of the souls in Purgatory, will hasten their release, so that like birds released from a cage they may fly to heaven to the very arms of the loving God. If I may give physical help to my friends on earth who are bound to me by ties of earthly love, why cannot we who are members of the same Mystical Body and are bound by the immortal ties of the charity of the Spirit of Christ, relieve the burdens of the souls in Purgatory? We are all one in Christ, and though our deeds be small, our alms be trivial, our mortification be slight, they take on added virtue and efficacy when united in Holy Mass with the Sacrifice of Calvary; for then the Father in Heaven sees not us but His beloved Son offering the all-pleasing oblation for those who are beloved of us.

Such is the Communion of Saints, the doctrine of the solidarity of the faithful in the Mystical Body of Christ. It takes us out of this tiny universe of ours with its insignificant distance of millions of light years; it transports us out of the narrowness of nationalities, the boundaries of internationalism, the confining limits of space and the servitude of time, into that eternal kingdom which has neither past nor future where Abraham, Isaac, and Jacob live with Peter, Joan of Arc, and the Little Flower, where the soldiers on earth breathe the same atmosphere of charity as the souls in heaven, where the same blood pulsates through every cell of the great Mystical Body in heaven, on earth, and in Purgatory, because all are in Christ Jesus our Head.

Never does the Christian stand alone. Beneficent influences from the past, like the sun from another world, are pouring out upon his soul; powerful streams of living waters from the eternal are renewing his spiritual youth like the eagle's; mysterious forces of invisible might, issuing forth from his fellow soldiers in the militant Church, are magnetizing him into greater apostolic zeal for the cause of Christ. Everywhere there is communion, traffic, exchange of prayers, merits, sacrifices.

What a relief to belong to another society where men do not talk of their plans of tomorrow, and their little sand castles which the waves of time will wash up on the shore of a dying world, but where we can live, move, and breathe in that infinite realm where we may begin and break off; sow and let others reap; execute and let others complete; lay the foundation and let others build thereon—because Rome is eternal, because victory is assured, because Christ is King, who has overcome the world.

Blind indeed would be he who thought the good he accomplished for the Church was the fruit of his own effort. And on this point permit a personal remark. I live under no illusions. If these radio talks and those of the past have been successful in bringing souls to Christ, as they have done, it is not because I preached them. It is because there poured in upon me from you, members of the Communion of Saints, your petitions, your sacrifices, your prayers. And so let me say to you now while on the subject—thanks and God bless you!

THE SPIRITUAL BETHLEHEM

DELIVERED ON MARCH 24, 1935

THUS far we have considered at some length how Christ prolongs His Incarnation in His Mystical Body, the Church. But little or nothing has been said of the role played by His Blessed Mother in that new Body. This is because her importance is such that it deserves a special consideration.

Some dim suggestion and hint of the part Mary plays in the regeneration of the human race is to be found in the part Eve played in its fall. Sacred Scripture tells us that Christ is the second Adam who, by His obedience on the tree of the cross, undid the disobedience of the first Adam under the tree of knowledge of good and evil. If Christ is the spiritual counterpart of Adam and the new head of the human race, then Mary, the mother of those who live in Christ, is the counterpart of Eve, the mother of those who died in Adam. A fitting parallel indeed, for if woman played such an important role in the fall of the human race, then it is fitting that her role be no less important in its redemption. In a word, Mary is the Mother of the Mystical Body of Christ, the Church.

In order to understand how literal and real this truth is dwell for a moment on the primary fact that Mary is the Mother of Christ. He who from all eternity was begotten of the Father, is generated in terms of the Blessed Mother without man, but by the overshadowing of the Holy Spirit. Her life from that point on is inseparably bound up with His; never does Scripture mention her apart from Him. She is with her divine Son in the flight into

Egypt; she is with Him in the Temple praying the perfect prayer to the Heavenly Father; she is with Him during His labors and years of obedience in the humble Nazarene home; she is with Him in His preaching; and stands at the foot of the cross as He dies for the redemption of the world.

Such beautiful devotion makes her the loveliest of all the lovely mothers of the world, the paragon of maternity, and the prototype of motherhood. But this does not tell the whole truth concerning Mary. She was more than the mother of the physical Christ. If her divine Son were only a man, then her maternity might be purely a corporal one. But recall that her Son is the Son of God as well as the Son of Man. Recall furthermore that during His earthly life He promised to assume a new body after His Ascension into heaven, a body which would be made up of the countless faithful who believed in Him, and through which body would flow His life and truth and love, like the sap of the vine flows through the branches. Once He ascended into heaven it was no longer possible for His physical body to grow and develop, for it possessed the fruits of glory. But the other body which He assumed on Pentecost, which is His church, *could* grow and develop. He said it would grow like the mustard seed, and St. Paul building on that thought, speaks of it as the "increase of God."

This means that in addition to the physical Christ, whose life began at Bethlehem and ended with the Ascension, there is also the mystical Christ which began with Pentecost and which will endure through all eternity. Now if the fullness of Christ embraces not only His historical life in Galilee but also His mystical life in the Church, then should not Mary be not only the Mother of the physical Christ but also the Mother of the fullness of Christ, or the Mother of the Church? The Mother of Jesus should therefore be our Mother, otherwise the whole Christ would not be entirely the Son of Mary. She would be His Mother in the physical sense but she would not be His Mother in the mystical sense. She would be the Mother of the Head but she would not be the Mother of His Body. This could hardly be, for the sun which shines on the vine to give it strength also gives strength to the branches; it must be that she who is the Mother of the Vine, which is the natural Christ, is also the Mother of the branches, which are the Church. As the Mystical Body is the complement and fullness of the natural Body of Christ, so too the divine motherhood of the Head should be complemented and have its fullness in the motherhood of the Mystical Body. Since she co-operated in the Incarnation by her consent she should also co-operate in the prolongation of the Incarnation, or the Church.

Would there not have been a great lacuna in what we receive from our divine Savior if He had not given His Mother to us as our Mother? Think of all the other heavenly benefits He gave us, and then ask yourself why He should stop short of giving us as mother the woman whom He chose above all the women of the earth as the spotless portal of the flesh through which He came to us in the form and image of man. He gave us His Heavenly Father and taught us to pray to Him as "Our Father"; He gave us His Body and His Blood in the Eucharist as pledge of everlasting life; He gave us His Spirit to "teach us all truth"; He gave us the fruits of His Resurrection and Ascension, raising us to "sit together in the heavenly places"; He gave us His victory over sin by making us heirs of heaven; He gave us His sonship by calling us to be adopted sons as He is the natural Son; He gave us His life that we might live in Him.

Now if His Mother were not given, then He has not been the perfect Lover who gives all. If His testament does not include the

FULTON J. SHEEN

gift of His Mother, then has He a right to exclaim from the cross, "It is finished"? Can all be finished if there is yet one omission? Did He not say He would not leave us orphans? But would we not be orphans without a mother? If He emptied His generous Heart by giving us His Father, His life, His Spirit, then why should His arm be shortened in holding back His Mother? He called us to be His brothers, and adopted sons of the Heavenly Father. But if He has a Mother should not we who are His brothers also have the same Mother? Grace is the perfection of nature, and if in the natural order we receive natural life through a woman, why should we not also receive supernatural life? Once granted He has given us His Mother as our Mother, then how true ring His words: "And all my things are thine, and thine are mine."

What we would expect Him to do as befitting His divine love, He has actually done. Note how Sacred Scripture, at first implicity, and then explicity, reveals how Mary is the Mother of the Church. It will be recalled that St. Luke in recounting the birth of our Lord says that Mary brought forth her "first born." Certain carnal-minded critics have argued that this meant our Lady had other children according to the flesh, quite ignoring the fact that the Scriptures clearly indicate she was a virgin. The statement "first born" may indeed mean that Mary was to have other children, but not by the flesh, only by the Spirit. It suggests that she was to have a spiritual progeny which would make up the Mystical Body of Her divine Son, just as Eve is called the "mother of all living," to designate her as the mother of men in the natural order. Sara gave only one son to Abraham, the father of believers, and yet she is called the mother of all Israel. So there is a clear suggestion in the words "first born" that she who begot corporally the Head of the Church was also to beget spiritually its members. Since the Head and the Body are inseparable it is therefore true to say that when Mary bore Christ in her womb she was virtually carrying the whole Mystical Body. The mother earth which bears the vine also bears the branches.

For a proof of this we need only look to Pentecost, when the risen Savior poured forth the merits of His redemption by sending His Spirit upon the Apostles to make them His new Body of which He, at the right hand of the Father, was the glorious Head. But our Lord did not assume His Mystical Body on Pentecost without the co-operation of His Blessed Mother. If our poor intellects thought out the Redemption and the sanctification of the world, we would have planned to have our Lord take His Mother with Him to heaven on Ascension Thursday; we would have thought it becoming that her work was done, once Easter gave the victory of life over death. But not so with divine wisdom. Her divine Son willed that since she was the nurse and mother of the physical Body with which He redeemed the world, so she should be left behind to be the nurse and mother of His Mystical Body with which He would pour forth the fruits of the redemption upon the souls of men. As she had been the Mother of the Head, so she should be the Mother of the Body.

Ten days after the Ascension we find the Apostles "persevering with one mind in prayer with Mary the Mother of Jesus," awaiting the descent of the Holy Spirit. The Spirit had descended upon her at Nazareth to make her the Mother of Jesus; now He descends upon the Apostles to make them His new Body and her the Mother of that Body. Virgin in the flesh she brought forth her first-born, Christ, virgin by the purity of her faith she brings forth her other-born, the Church—and in both instances it is the Holy Spirit which renders her fecund.

Such was God's reason for leaving the Blessed Mother on earth for a time after Her Son had ascended into heaven. Called to the sublime vocation of being the Mother of Christ in His Redemptive work, it was her duty not only to cradle the Head of the Church in Bethlehem, but also to cradle the Body in Jerusalem. The Mystical Body of Pentecost, like the physical body of Bethlehem, was small and delicate and frail, like any new-born thing. Its members were small; its organs were in the process of formation, and though life was there it was yet to grow in "age and grace and wisdom before God and men." But that growth and development could not be without the menace of hatred and persecution; for new Herods would arise to attack the Church as the other Herod had attacked its Head.

It was necessary, therefore, that the Mother of the infant Mystical Christ be there to bestow her loving care on it as thirty-three years before she had watched over the infant Christ. Every infant needs a mother's care—even an infant Church. The mystery of Jesus did not begin without her, neither would it finish without her. Our blessed Lord had kept His promise. He did not leave us orphans. He gave us His Father as our Father, His Spirit as our Spirit, and His Mother as our Mother.

Not only was it fitting that Mary be present as Mother at the birth of the Mystical Christ, it was also fitting that she be present as Queen of the Apostles on the solemn day when the Church began preaching the Gospel to the world.

From the very beginning she was the Apostle *par excellence* of Her divine Son. She it was who first made Jesus known to His precursor John the Baptist on the occasion of her visit to Elizabeth; she it was who first made Jesus known to the Jews in the person of the shepherds, and to the Gentiles in the person of the Wise Men. It was therefore in keeping with her vocation that she be with the Apostles on Pentecost to make known the Mystical Christ to the world, as she had made known the physical Christ to shepherds and kings. She gave birth to Him, who came to cast fire on earth and willed that it be enkindled, and her role would now have been incomplete if she had not been in the very center of the tongues of fire which the Spirit of her Son sent upon the Apostles to make them burn with His message even to the consummation of the world.

Pentecost was Mary's spiritual Bethlehem, her new Epiphany in which, as Mother, standing by the crib of the Mystic Christ, she makes Him known once again to other shepherds and other Kings.

Finally when in the Providence of God the Church had grown to its full stature and began its "public life," as her Son began His when He left the maternal home at Nazareth, Mary was called home to her reward. Her divine Son had His Crucifixion and His Resurrection and then His Ascension. Mary had her crucifixion as the sword of sorrow pierced her heart on Calvary. But she was now to have the counterpart of His Ascension—and that was her Assumption into Heaven.

In that state of glory for which we labor here below, Christ the Head of the Mystical Body lives to intercede for us before the heavenly Father. Associated with Him in glory, as she had been associated with Him in His earthly pilgrimage, is His Mother, the Queen of Angels and Saints. Inseparably united at the cross when the reservoirs of Redemption were filled, they are now inseparably united in heaven as those same merits are poured out upon all who believe in Him as Brother, in her as Mother, and in God as Father.

He is the Redeemer, she the co-Redemptrix. "Christ is the Head of the Church; Mary the channel therein of Christ's graces. All benefits, all graces, all heavenly favors come from Christ as from a Head. All descend into the Body of the Church through

Mary, as through the neck of the human body the head vivifies the members" (Bellarmine). "Every grace given to the world comes by three steps in perfect order; from the Father to Christ; from Christ to the Virgin; from the Virgin to us" (Encyclical *Magnae Dei Matris*). The role of Mary in the Church is therefore just as active as her role in the Incarnation.

How could we fail to love her whom our Lord loved so much? It is impossible to love Christ adequately without also loving the Mother who gave Him to us. Those who begin by ignoring her, soon end by ignoring Him—for the two are inseparable in the great drama of Redemption. Hence the Church from the day of Pentecost has been most zealous in defending her honor and her purity, praising her for giving a Savior to the world.

Not only does the Mystical Body as a whole honor Mary, but each honors her as Mother, for she is the Mother of all only because she is the Mother of each of us. It is absolutely impossible to convey to anyone outside the Church the filial devotion we bear that sweet Mother of Mothers. As children who wish to influence their father go to their mother to intercede for them, so do we go to Mary.

When the wine of your life is failing and your faith is weak, and your charity growing cold, go to her who at Cana's feast interceded to her divine Son for the replenishing of the wine of gladness. When your whole frame racks beneath the tempter fly to the patronage of her Immaculate Heart, whose heel crushes the head of the serpent. When the cold hand of death is laid upon those whom you love, and your heart seems torn in twain, climb to the Hill of Calvary to be consoled by the Mother of Sorrows who is also the Cause of Our Joy. When sin corrodes your soul and rusts your heart and you are weary without God, then have recourse to Mary the Refuge of Sinners, for she, the

Sinless One, knows what sin is—for she too lost her God. When the sweet inspirations of the Holy Spirit call you away from the passing tin and tinsel of earthly joys to the life of sanctity, then pray to her that you may follow her dictates to love Her divine Son: "Whatsoever he shall say to you, do ye." Never was it known that anyone who fled to her protection, or asked her help, was left unaided. She is our advocate before the Father. Until eternity dawns you who live in the hope of that eternal union with the Daughter of the Father, the Mother of the Son, and the Spouse of the Holy Ghost, pray from the bottom of your hearts that prayer which is the counterpart of the Our Father, the prayer of the children of Mary, and say to her:

"Hail Mary, full of grace, the Lord is with thee. Blessed art thou amongst women, and blessed is the fruit of thy womb, Jesus. Holy Mary, Mother of God, pray for us sinners, now and at the hour of our death. Amen."

THE SACRIFICE OF THE MASS

DELIVERED ON MARCH 31, 1935

WHATEVER we may say of the world and its wickedness, there is nevertheless hidden in the heart of it the beautiful instinct to remember those who died in sacrifice. Every nation under the sun has its memorial day consecrated to the blessed memory of the heroes of its battles and its wars. Now, if there be such a remembered gratitude for those who died for a nation, why should there not be a memorial for Him who died for the world; if we remember those who sacrificed themselves for others, why should we not remember Him from whose death all sacrifice has received its sacred seal and noble inspiration? Calvary is too beautiful to be lost! The cross bearing the burden of the Savior of men is too holy to be forgotten! "Greater love than this no man hath that he lay down his life for his friends." Such love deserves to be perpetuated.

Lest men should forget—and how quickly they do—Our Lord resolved to institute a memorial of His sacrifice. Most men at the approach of death prepare their last wills and testaments, in which they dispose of their properties, their titles, their wealth. On the eve of His death our Lord made His Last will and testament but, unlike men, He left that which no man on dying ever left—namely, Himself.

This He could do, being God. He would leave Himself not in any indifferent act of His life, but in that supreme act where love reached its peak in the sacrifice of Good Friday. The particular means He chose to represent the awful separation of His Blood from His Body on the cross were under the symbols of bread and wine. Gathering His Apostles about Him in the upper room on the night that has since been called Holy Thursday, He anticipated the sacrifice of the cross which would follow in less than eighteen hours. By the separate consecration of first the bread and then the wine He symbolically represented His future crucifixion in which His Body as Bread of Heaven, and His Blood as the Wine of Life, were to be separated one from the other for the redemption of the world. He was thus offering up what was in store for Him; anticipating, as it were, His Baptism of Blood by pledging Himself to death in the sight of His Father and men. Everyone knows the circumstances of that evening. He took bread in His hand "and blessed and broke; and gave to his disciples, and said: Take ye and eat. This is my body. And taking the chalice, he gave thanks, and gave to them, saying: Drink ye all of this. For this is my blood of the new testament, which shall be shed for many unto remission of sins."

Then looking forward to all ages and all times, and to all hearts who would ever crave a memorial of the death which gave us everlasting life, He said, "Do this for a commemoration of me."

The next afternoon at three o'clock that which He anticipated and foreshadowed and mystically represented in the Last Supper, came to pass: His Body was delivered to executioners, His Blood was poured forth.

Now, here we are nineteen hundred years removed from that Last Supper and that crimsoned Golgotha. Keeping both in mind and the fact that He the God-man begged us to remember His last will and testament, cast your eyes about the world and ask yourself these questions: Who have done that which He asked us to do the night of the Last Supper in commemoration of Him? Who have taken bread and wine into their hands and by the mystical sword of the words of consecration symbolically represented the separation of both on a cross, where Love sank to the depths and arose as Sacrifice? Who have a daily memorial ceremony in which there is re-enacted, in an unbloody manner, the tragedy of Calvary?

For answer enter into any Catholic church in the world and during the early morning hours you will see a priest, whose heritage is one with those of the Upper Room, mount an altar, take bread and wine in his hands, breathe over them the very words of our Lord Himself, and as a bell tinkles and hundreds of heads in the Church bow in prayer, you will see the priest kneel in adoration of the bread which is the Body and the wine which is the Blood of our Lord and Savior; and as both are lifted above his head, as the cross was lifted above the earth, you will understand how that same Lord erects Calvary once again amidst hearts which love and hands which crucify. Someone has remembered His words. "Do this for a commemoration of me" has not fallen on deaf ears. Calvary was too beautiful to be forgotten. It is remembered! It is commemorated! It is re-enacted! It is re-presented! It is prolonged through space and time—and its memorial is the Mass.

There is grave danger that we may believe the Mass to be only a memorial ceremony such as that we have on Memorial Day for our hero soldiers, or as a kind of imitation of the Last Supper on the stage of the altar in which we are passive spectators; or as a prayer in which there is only a repetition of the beautiful words of the Last Supper. No! The Mass is none of these things. *The Mass is the Sacrifice of the Mystical Body of Christ, and is one with Calvary, which was the sacrifice of the physical body of Christ.*

The Mass is a supra-temporal reality, by which the glorified Christ in Heaven prolongs His sacrifice on the cross by and through us. Though He is priest and victim the manner of offering is not the same in both the Mass and the cross. On the cross He was alone; in the Mass He is with us. On the cross He offered up His life for all who would one day be incorporated to His Mystical Body; in the Mass He renews the sacrifice for all who are actually incorporated into that Mystical Body. On the cross the historical Christ offered Himself, in the Mass the mystical Christ (which is Christ *and* us) offers Himself. The cross was in Jerusalem as a space, and it was nineteen hundred years ago as a time; the Mass is the same cross made actual throughout space and time. There is no time or space between Calvary and now. On the cross the human nature of Christ was susceptible of suffering; in the Mass His human nature is glorified and hence He cannot suffer except through other human natures which make up His Mystical Body. The cross purchases Redemption; the Mass applies it. The Mass is the tremendous experience of the reality of Golgotha with its forgiveness and its love, its power and its pardon, extended and prolonged even unto this hour.

The Mass, I say, is the sacrifice of the Mystical Body, the Church, and not a mere empty symbolism of Calvary. On the cross, our Lord took the human nature which He assumed from His Mother in the unity of His Person and, as priest on the cross, offered it to His Father in reparation for the sins of men. That human nature after the Resurrection and Ascension was elevated to the glory of heaven. The human nature of Jesus can therefore never suffer again. It has entered into its reward beyond all crucifixions and deaths. "Christ rising again from the dead, dieth now no more, death shall no more have dominion over him."

FULTON J. SHEEN

He can therefore add nothing to His priestly office except by and through us. And it is this he has chosen to do. He wills to do with other human natures scattered throughout the world, what He did with His own human nature taken from His Virgin Mother. He, therefore, as Head of the Mystical Body in heaven, calls others to Himself—other Peters, Pauls, Johns, Marthas, Marys, Thereses, Augustines, Cyrils, Boscos, Little Flowers, in a word, all the millions of baptized men and women who have been incorporated to Him by Baptism—as His new Mystical Body. He asks them to give Him their human natures in love, that He may continue His redemptive priesthood by and through them, so that not only He in His own human nature, but *He in ours*, may offer them anew to His Heavenly Father in an unending act of priestly sacrifice. As a great patriot in time of national crisis seeks not only to offer his own life for the sake of his country, but also strives to rally others to himself that, through their corporate selflessness, the whole nation may be preserved, so He, the glorified Christ in heaven, seeks the enlistment of you and me—all of us—under His headship, that we may offer ourselves *with* His offering on the cross, to win the triumphs of other loving Calvaries, even as He.

This enlistment takes place at the offertory of the Mass where we are present under the form of bread and wine. Just as bread is one though it is made from a multiplicity of grains of wheat, just as wine is one though made from a multiplicity of grapes, so we are one in Christ though a multiplicity of cells in the Mystical Body. Furthermore, bread and wine represent the substantial nourishment of life. The grain of wheat which is the fat of the land, and the grape which is the marrow and blood of the earth, are fundamental means of renewing man's substance and refreshing his blood. When therefore man brings bread and wine to the altar (or their equivalent, that which purchases them) he is equivalently bringing himself.

If there is anything which adequately describes the part of the faithful in the Offertory of the Mass, it is the picture of our Lord standing on the hill of Calvary before His great cross. Crowded about Him on the same hill we stand with our little crosses stretched on the ground alongside His great model cross. The very moment He makes the offertory of His life, and walks to His cross to prove that His love for us is stronger than death, we walk to our little crosses, make the offertory of our lives in union with Him, to prove that our love of righteousness, of justice, of truth, of love, and of God, is stronger than our love of that life which quickly passes away.

A few minutes later comes the awful mystery of the consecration, in which the priest by the separate consecration of bread and wine renews in an unbloody manner the immolation of Christ on His cross. When the priest, in obedience to the command of our Lord at the Last Supper to "do this for a commemoration of me," pronounces the words over the bread, "This is my body," and over the wine, "This is my blood," the primary significance of the words is that the substance of the bread is changed into the substance of the Body of our Lord, and the substance of the wine is changed into the substance of His Blood. Mystically divided by the separate consecration of the bread and wine, our Lord thus renews the sacrifice of Calvary's cross. But our Lord is not alone. Just as the Offertory of the Mass is the *offering* of Christ and us, so the consecration of the Mass is the *sacrifice* of Christ and us. The Vine sacrificed Himself on the cross; the Vine and the branches now sacrifice themselves in the Mass. The primary meaning of the words of Consecration then refers to the Vine: this is the Body and this is the Blood of Christ, renewing the sacrifice of Calvary. But the secondary meaning refers to the branches united to the Vine to form the Mystical Body, in which Peter and Paul, Mary and Anne, and all members of the Church, say: "This is my body, this is my blood. I offered myself with thee at the Offertory; now I immolate myself with thee at the consecration. Take my body and my blood with thee to the cross; take my body and blood with all the pains, sorrows, agonies; with their capacities for love, for service, and for repentance; take them with thee to the cross, that they may be united with thy sacrifice which alone makes them acceptable to thy Heavenly Father; that they may purchase me to thyself in *act*, as thou didst purchase me in *hope* at Calvary. Take not merely my possessions, my titles, my apostolate, my zeal, my energy, but take all that I am, the very substance of my life—my body, my blood. Take them, make them one with thy sacrifice as the drop of water becomes one with the wine. Possess them so that what is mine is thine, so that the Heavenly Father in looking down upon thy renewed Calvary may find that there is but one Body and one Blood which is that of thee, His beloved Son, in whom the Father is well pleased."

On Calvary Christ was alone; in the Mass we are one with Him as the grains of wheat are one bread, and the grapes of the vine one wine. The Mass then is *Calvary recalled, renewed, and applied*—the only thing in this world which makes it possible for us to follow His command, "Take up your cross daily and follow me." In no other act of His Mystical Life does He come so close to us. Bethlehem is with us in the Real Presence; His voice is with us in the Church; His hands are with us in the Sacraments; but His love unto death is with us in the continued Sacrifice of the Mass.

Thanks to it Calvary is set up in our midst. Thanks to it we need not go back twenty centuries to the material cross, for our glory is not in the *material* cross on which our Lord suffered—rather it is the Spirit of that Sacrifice coming in power to him who has faith in Him, converting the body and soul into a sacrifice. The Mass is Calvary realized, made present, contemporized, lifted out of the limits of space and time, living in the members of the Mystical Body, sealing us, separating us from the world, sacrificing us, changing our crosses into crucifixes and making us so much one with Christ that the heavenly Father sees but Him whose sacrifice alone is acceptable and whose prayers alone are heard.

There are little children fresh from their First Communion, old men and women looking forward to eternal youth, young maidens pure as the Mother of their Savior, young seminarians looking forward to their first Mass, penitent sinners as late-season flowers offering the best that is left in their lives—and yet all these are but as one Bread and one Chalice, losing their individuality for the time being to be one with the Mystical Christ. Their sufferings and their pains, their disappointments and their poverty, their mental anguish and their tears, of and by themselves would make them pessimists. But now they are offered in the Mass, they have Christ's name stamped on them, and they become precious because part of His sacrifice. Only when they are "massed" in Calvary's sacrifice, do they become acceptable sacrifices; only when they are one with the cross do they become redeeming as the cross; only when they are crucified with Christ do they hold the pledge of His Resurrection. Hence the prayer of the Mass, said after the consecration:

"We humbly beseech thee, Almighty God, to command that these things—Christ's Body and Blood, as well as ourselves, our vows and prayers be borne by the hands of thy holy angel to thine altar on high, in sight of thy divine majesty, that so many of us as at this altar shall partake of and receive the Most Holy Body and Blood of thy divine Son, may be filled with every heavenly blessing and grace, through Christ our Lord. Amen."

* * *

REPARATION

DELIVERED ON APRIL 7, 1935

UNDER the title of reparation, this broadcast proposes to discuss the mutual relation existing between members of the Mystical Body. As St. Paul has put it: "There are many members indeed, yet one body." The unity which binds us together is closer than the unity which binds together the cells of a human body, because the principle of our unity is the Holy Spirit. Like a mighty river the Spirit of Love swells and sweeps through the souls of men, like the blood plasma sweeps through the human body, supplying potency to every unit, bathing it with nutriment, and baptizing it with power.

United as we are to one another in the Mystical Body of Christ, there is reciprocity, mutual sympathy, and a sense of cooperativeness between us. We should therefore feel responsible toward one another as the various parts of the human body feel responsible toward one another. "As the eye cannot say to the hand: I need not thy help: nor again the head to the feet: I have no need of you"; so neither can we dispense ourselves from other members of the Mystical Body regardless of how lowly their position, or regardless of how different their vocation.

Now of the various sympathies existing between us as members of the Mystical Body, I wish to mention three: sorrow, joy, and reparation.

Firstly, there is sorrow: If I hurt my hand, my whole body feels the pain—for my hand is one with my body. If my eye sees a blow about to be directed against the ear, the eye does not say:

FULTON J. SHEEN

"It is not going to strike me, and therefore I need not worry." As a matter of fact the eye does seek to prevent injury to the ear, for both are one because parts of the same organism. Now in the Mystical Body of Christ, the sorrow, the suffering, and the persecution of the Church in one part of the world should be felt by the Church in all parts of the world. On this logic the Church in Mexico, for example, is part of the Mystical Body as much as the arm is part of the human body. What it suffers, the whole Church should therefore feel as its own. As St. Paul has said: "If one member suffer anything, all the members suffer with it."

Now do we actually feel the sufferings of the Church in Mexico, or in Germany, as we should? Do we realize that we are one with them, because we are parts of the same body vivified by the same Spirit? Do we pray for them? Do we feel sad at the loss of that faith by those who once possessed it? Do we grieve for those who once loved God and then left the paths of peace? Do we who have some of the world's goods realize that the poor parts of this, our Body, have need of our superfluities? Do national boundaries blind our vision to that wider outlook where there is only that supranationalism which is the fatherhood of God and the brotherhood in Christ? When the Church is being persecuted in one part of the world, when churches are pillaged, bishops exiled, the faithful martyred, do we feel that their pain and their sorrow is ours, as much as the pain in the arm is the pain in the whole body? If we are insensitive to these sorrows of the Church in other parts of the world, then we are insensitive to our membership in the Mystical Body of Christ. Then we are calloused to those finer sympathies which prove not only that we are gentlemen but, what is more refined, Christians worthy of the name. The interaction of the moon on the tides, the sympathy between a baby's cry and the vibration of a distant

226

star, is as nought compared to that finer interaction and sympathy between Christian and Christian in the body of Christ which is His Church.

What is true of sorrow and pain in the Mystical Body is true also of its joy. In the human body if the tongue tastes something sweet the whole body rejoices. In like manner in the Church, St. Paul tells us, "if one member glory, all the members rejoice with it." When, therefore, the Church canonizes a saint, when there is an increase of communions in the Church, when sinners return to the faith and do penance which makes even the angels rejoice, when the spirit of prayer and contemplation grows in the souls of men as worldliness decreases, when foreign missionaries make new conquests for Christ—each of these should make us rejoice, for it is a joy of a part of our body.

If we rejoice, then, we are conscious of our solidarity in the Mystical Body of Christ; then we are prepared to understand not merely the *sympathy* we must have for the joys and sorrows of others, but also the *reparation*, we should offer for those members who stand in need of it.

The analogy of the human body makes clear this idea of reparation. It is a well-established fact that all the cells and nerves and organs of the body have their keyboard in the brain. The connection between the right hand and the left is not direct, but mediate—that is, it is established through the central nervous system. In the event of perfectly established and harmonious relations between the center and its members, there is a perfect unanimity and reciprocity between the members themselves, which guarantees mutual help and assistance. For example, let a speck of dust enter the eye and at once the hand flies up to minister. Let a man slip in the street and sprain his foot and the other foot will do double duty all the way home. If a person burnt his face, doctors would graft skin from another part of his body and apply it to his face; if a man is suffering from anemia, doctors will transfuse blood from another member of society to that weak individual, to cure him of that anemic condition. This fine fellowship and fealty springs out of perfectly sustained relations with the head.

Now in the Mystical Body all members who are one by obedience to the same visible head, can therefore be of service one to the other. If it is possible for the hand to help the eye, do you not think it possible for a Catholic in America to help a Catholic in India, because both are connected through the keyboard of the Vicar of Christ? If it is possible to graft skin, is it not also possible to graft prayer? If it is possible to transfuse blood, is it not also possible to transfuse sacrifice? This process of atoning and sacrificing ourselves for other members of the Mystical Body is what is known as reparation. Such is the meaning of the words of St. Paul: "Bear ye one another's burdens; so you also shall fulfill the law of Christ."

Such is the reason for the communities in the Church, such as the Carmelites and Poor Clares, the Trappists and the Chartreuse, and many others whose supreme business in life it is to repair the harm done by others, and to bring succor those who cannot help themselves. The world is full of those who sin and atone not; who offend God and never repent; who have their sins forgiven, but who never do penance. These poor, burnt, anemic, wounded members of the Mystical Body of Christ may yet be saved by those who out of their superfluities expend spiritual wealth for the salvation of souls. The world which asks of such saintly mortified souls hidden away in cloisters and convents: "What good do they do?"—fails to understand that in the order of divine life they are doing for the wounded on the spiritual battlefields of the Church, that which, in the order of human life, nurses and doctors are doing on the battlefields of the world. And since the saving of a soul is immeasurably more important than the saving of a body, we may very well ask if the comparison is justified at all.

In these days when the world regards a sin as a lesser evil than a headache, the value of reparation in the Mystical Body is apt to be overlooked. It needs to be repeated that reparation exists because there is sin. In every sin there is a double element: the joy of a forbidden fruit and the act of disobedience against God. Equilibrium can be established between the two, therefore, only by a commensurate pain to atone for the forbidden joy, and a compensating repentance to atone for the act of disobedience. Of these two elements the latter is more important, for it gives to the first its moral significance. Otherwise pain would be pain for the sake of pain, and not sacrifice. Then we would be like the Hindu mystics who glorify suffering as an end in itself. It is the sorrow, the contrition, and the desire to love God which changes pain into sacrifice for what is pain but sacrifice without love?

But it is not enough to be sorry for our sins. Sin involves a debt, and the debt must be paid. It is not sufficient for a man who has run into great debt to say to his creditors: "I am very sorry I have contracted such debts. I will not run up any more in the future." He must *pay the debts* in addition to being contrite. So likewise with sin. It is not enough to tell God we are sorry for our sins; we must pay the debts contracted by them—and if there was fun in running them up, there must be pain in tracking them down. If we take a hundred steps in the wrong direction, we must put our foot down one hundred times to get back in the right direction. Where there was forbidden joy, there must be willing sacrifice. If we sow cockle in joy with our wheat, we must pluck it out in pain. There is no pardon without reparation. That is why beneath all the liturgical difference of all peoples, there has always been sacrifice. They have testified with Paul that "without shedding of blood there is no remission."

Thus it is by reparation for others that we "fill up those things that are wanting of the sufferings of Christ, in my flesh, for his Body which is the church." This means that the redemption of the physical body of Christ is complete, but not the redemption of His Mystical Body.

The cross, then, is the focal point of all creation. Creation was only a prelude to the drama of Calvary. Creation exists for no other reason than to have a cross erected upon it. And the inspiration of the Sacrifice of the cross was love wherein God who loves man poured out the crushed-out sweetness of His Sacred Heart. Love is the reason of all reparation, for love by its nature means *not* to have, to own, to possess, but to be had, to be owned, to be possessed.

That is why love always expresses itself in terms of arrows and darts—something that wounds. Its greatest luxury is to spend; its greatest joy is to serve; its keenest pleasure is to throw itself on the altar of sacrifice for the one loved. That is why St. Augustine could exclaim: "Give me a heart that has really loved, and I will tell him what God is." Every human heart that has ever been in love, or has ever risen one step above the modern wallowing in sex, knows this. And yet these revealing moments when your heart stands naked before you, and you saw its authentic fires, are but poor and partial reflections of the great Sun of Love which is God. There is not a mother in the world whose white passion of love swings open the great portals of flesh to bring into the world the self-gift of a child; there is not a father in the world who has thought his highest heaven on earth to bear a cross for that child; there is not a saint on earth whose passionless passion for souls has not, like a pelican, wounded itself to nourish with its merits the fledglings of Christ's flock; in a word, there has never been a heart that ever beat once in sacrificing love—which did not understand that since God is love, He should fittingly overflow the boundaries of heaven, and from the cross reach into a wounded side to give us the hostage of His Sacred Heart.

THE BROKEN HEART

DELIVERED ON APRIL 14, 1935

TODAY ushers us into the week called Holy and the Friday called Good, when mankind nailed its Redeemer to the cross. The details of that redeeming death we are reserving for our broadcast on Good Friday night. For the moment our only purpose is to prepare the way for that broadcast with a few thoughts on the broken heart. As Adam slept, God took from out his side his spouse Eve, the mother of all the living in the order of the flesh. As Christ slept in death on the cross, He took from out His side His Spouse the Church, the Mother of all the living in the order of the spirit. The Church, the Mystical Body of Christ, was therefore born of the broken heart of God made man.

The physical sufferings of our Lord were more intense than those of men for all time, because His organism was more sensitive and delicate, and therefore the more responsive to pain. The mental sufferings of our Lord were more intense than the combined mental sufferings of all men, because He was God and knew all. Therefore nothing came to Him by surprise; He suffered every pain before it came, because He knew beforehand that it was coming. Not only that, He offered Himself wholly and entirely as a holocaust, not as one who could not prevent the pain, but as one who could have prevented it and still accepted it freely, absolutely, and resolutely. His suffering was greater because as God He had a greater power of realizing it. And this is precisely what He meant when He said: "My soul is sorrowful even unto death."

But it is not on His physical or His mental sufferings that I would dwell but rather on something about which we so seldom think, namely, His broken heart. In order that we may understand it, let me ask you to consider a pain inflicted on you by one whom you love dearly. The barbed shaft of the unkind word of your enemy would wound but would it be comparable to the unkind word of one whom you loved? In the latter case, it would not be the bitter word that pained you; it would be rather that he whom you loved did it; it would not be the thing that was said, but rather the person who said it. Is it not clear then that pain increases in direct ratio and proportion with the love we have for those who inflict it? Is it not also true that what adds to the grief is that those who wound us, should be so unconscious of our love? A father, for example, sees his son squandering his substance, weakening his will by repeated sins, and degrading his body by crime and dissipation, and above all else by losing his faith. The grief of the father is intensified not only because of the love he bears his son, but also because the son is so indifferent to the hurt. The father is twice wounded: because he loves his son so much, and again because the son is so unmindful of it all. Was it not just that sense of wounded love, rather than a wounded body, that made Caesar cry out in sad surprise to his friend: "And thou, too, Brutus?"

Now to apply this to our Lord. His greatest suffering was not that nails should make His hands and feet red rivers of blood; not that thorns should encircle His brow with the crimson drops of the rosary of redemption; not that thirst should dry up the lips that preached the waters of everlasting life; not even that Mary's heart should be pierced through with Eden's transplanted sword, as His own body was fixed to Eden's transplanted tree. The greatest sorrow of Calvary was not that bronzed executioners shook dice as they watched Him die… All this was bearable…tolerable…and even understandable. "Forgive them for they know not what they do." But what was hard and unbearable and intolerable was that they whom He loved should do it! It was not that He should be betrayed, but that Judas whom He loved, should be the one to blister His lips; it was not that He should be crucified, but that His own friends should have demanded it; it was not that He should be denied, but that Peter, the rock, should do it; it was not the cross which struck Him the cruelest blow, it was that those whom He loved should have reared it; it was not so much that they wounded Him, but that they were so unconscious of it all; it was not so much the hurt, it was rather that they were so oblivious of their sin; it was not only because He loved us so much, but because we should hardly seem to care. That is the tragedy of Good Friday. The pain in itself was intense; but it became crucifying because it was inflicted by those whom He so deeply treasured. It was therefore not only His bleeding body which caused His death; it was also a broken heart—the rupture of a heart through the rapture of wounded love.

This thought of wounded love is behind the words of our Lord spoken by the psalmist: "If my enemy had reviled me, I would verily have borne with it… But thou…my guide, my familiar, who didst take sweetmeats together with me." If only the wounds were inflicted by enemies! But no! As He shows them His wounds He says with poignancy: "With these I was wounded in the house of them that loved me."

"Greater love than this no man hath, that he should lay down his life for his friends." And we may add, greater pain than this no man hath, that his friends should be so indifferent of His love. Such is the hidden tragedy of the broken heart of Christ.

Now as we enter into Holy Week when God is so merciful,

and above all times wills not the death of the sinner, but that he should be converted and live, what appeal could more move us than the appeal of the broken heart? I think the experience of most of us will verify this fact, that when we have deeply wounded another, what draws us back to him is not so much the wound itself, nor because we inflicted it, but rather because that person continued to love us even while His wounds were open and while we were so unconscious of His love. A little child who speaks disrespectfully to his mother, does not repent as quickly with a reprimand, as he does at her affectionate glance from tear-filled eyes revealing the wounded love of her broken heart. So, too, it is with our Lord. I should think that no appeal to sinners during this week could be more soul-stirring and more provocative of good than the thought that the crucified Savior loves them from the cross they themselves have carpentered, and looks at them kindly through eyes they would have filled with dust, and speaks to them through lips they burned with vinegar and gall. A man who has led a very wicked life, and who can be moved by no other appeal, is not unlikely to reform at the sight of his mother dying of a broken heart; in like manner we too who are sinners should be most moved to penitence and sorrow at the sight of our Savior dying of a broken heart. That He should say to me: "I forgive you, for you know not what you do"; that He should show me His wounds and say: "These I received from you, whom I call friend"; that He should not only say, "Forgive your enemies," but even forgive me the greatest of all; that He should love me, who am not worthy of being loved; in a word, that His Sacred Heart should be broken because of my hardheartedness—that is an appeal which no man worthy of the name can resist, and yet such is the appeal of Calvary and the cross.

And yet there are some who do resist! There are some hearts harder than the heart of the rocks beneath the cross which were broken when touched by His redeeming blood; there are some hearts colder than the executioners who stood within a stone's throw of the great drama of redemption and shook dice for the garments of God. Why must there be hearts who will love everything but Love? Money is loved! Power is loved! The passing show of the world is loved! But why should divine Love of all things be the great Unloved? Why should there be souls who, when God comes to earth, give Him a cross? Why should there be wounded wings that will not accept the healing of His hand? No wonder His heart broke! Fittingly indeed did the soldier Longinus ride beneath the cross, and with a lance pierce His side! That broken heart must not be hidden. All men must know that God loves them in their hate. It must stand revealed at the open door of His side that all men might know that through that portal, as through the portal of Noah's ark, we enter to be saved from the flood-waters of the sin and loneliness of the world.

Oh, would we but realize that we live in a world of broken hearts. We are victims of a shattered love; we are kings in exile; we are lovers looking for love. The very shape of our heart attests it. Our heart is not perfect in shape and contour like a valentine heart; there is a small piece missing out of the side of every human heart. That may be to symbolize a piece that we tore out of the heart of universal humanity on the cross. But the real meaning is this: As God made each human heart He kept a small sample of it in Heaven to be the heart of His divine Son made man who would die on the cross. We therefore can never love anyone with our *whole* heart, because we have not a *whole* heart—we have only a part of it. The rest of it is in the heart of the great Unloved on the cross. In Him alone therefore do we find that other part of our poor heart which makes us whole-hearted lovers. And that is how we heal the broken heart of Christ!

THE SEVEN LAST WORDS

DELIVERED ON GOOD FRIDAY, 1935

Introduction

Our Lord is the only King who ever stumbled to His throne. But that was because He is God, and God reveals His power through the weakness of a crucifixion and His wisdom through the foolishness of a cross.

Once on the heights of Calvary, where meet the crossroads of three civilizations in whose name He is crucified, He is fittingly stripped of His garments. They belong to His times, to Judea, to Galilee, to a small province of Rome. Now in order that He might not be localized by garments, but universalized as redeemer of the world, He permits Himself to be shorn of the last vestige of earthly things so as to be utterly and absolutely the poor man of the world.

What message will the King deliver from his unkingly throne? Last words are always important, but particularly the last words of Him who gave His life for the redemption of many. It will be recalled that one day the Apostles approached Him saying: "Lord, teach us to pray." He answered their request by giving them the perfect prayer: the "Our Father." Now the time comes for Him to say His own "Our Father." As there were seven petitions in the "Our Father" He taught us, so there are seven petitions in His own last prayer. They are known as the "Seven Last Words." We shall meditate conjointly on our "Our Father" and His "Our Father."

THE CHRIST

First Word

"Our Father who art in heaven."
"Father, forgive them for they know not what they do."

The first petition of the Our Father our Lord taught us was the prayer of priestly intercession: "Our Father Who art in heaven." The first word from the cross was the intercessory prayer of the perfect Priest: "Father forgive them for they know not what they do."

The Priest whence all priesthood is derived once asked us to look up to our Father Who is in Heaven. Now He begs that same Father to blot out the sins of those who crucify Him and to forgive them "for they know not what they do." He was finding an excuse for sins. He was telling His Father that we crucified Him only because of our ignorance. If we knew what we were doing, we would never have denied the Father in Heaven. Salvation is possible only because of our ignorance of how good God the Father is to send His only begotten Son into the world that we might have life in His name.

When our enemies crucify us, we say: "They should have known better." When we crucified Him, He said: "Forgive them, for they know not what they do." We love those who love us and honor those who flatter us; He loved those who hated Him and forgave even the hands that drove the nails. He loves not only the lovable, as we do—He loves also the hateful, which we are. That is why there is hope for us! "Our Father Who art in heaven, forgive us for we know not what we do."

FULTON J. SHEEN

Second Word

"Hallowed be thy name."
"Amen, I say to thee, this day thou shalt be with me in paradise."

God's name is hallowed by the recognition of His power and glory. The thief recognized God's power despite His powerlessness; and God's glory despite His defeat.

Picture two scenes as this second word is being spoken. On opposite sides of Sion there were men hanging on trees. On one side of the hill Judas was hanging from a tree; on the opposite side hung our Lord between two thieves. Note the difference in attitude of Judas and the thief on the right. Both were thieves. But there was this difference. Judas thought God's glory was purely external, manifested by earthly pomp and circumstance. Hence when he saw our Lord go down to defeat he sold Him for thirty pieces of silver. The thief on the left of our Lord was like Judas. He too felt the only power worth having was the power of saving him from pain. Hence he cried in agony: "Save thyself and us." In other words, do something external. But the thief on the right moved his pain-racked head toward our Lord, saw Him divested of every robe of royalty, and denuded of every badge of kingship. And yet he perceived the gold beneath the dust, and the kingdom through a cloud, and power to save a soul beneath the weakness of a drained body: "Lord, remember me when thou shalt come into thy Kingdom."

Our blessed Savior was so pleased to find His name hallowed amidst blasphemy, and His blessing recognized amidst curses, that He granted the humble prayer of the thief: "Amen, I say to thee, this day thou shalt be with me in Paradise."

The world is full of Judases who think the name of God is hallowed only by worldly pomp and splendor. They forget that the Kingdom of God is internal and "cometh not by observation," and that the Church which is the Mystical Christ manifests her greatest strength in the forgiveness of sins.

The world asks: "How can man forgive sin?" It might just as well ask how could a man whose kingdom is no wider than a beam of wood promise the kingdom of heaven to a thief.

The forgiveness of sin is a greater manifestation of the Power of God than the creation of the world. Creation makes something out of nothing. Forgiveness puts something into nothing. But the forgiveness which opens Paradise is obtained as the thief obtained his, namely by asking for it. Pardon, like all gifts of God, is conditioned. The latch on the door of divine forgiveness is on the inside of our soul—on *our* side, not on God's side. "Behold, I stand at the door and knock." He knocks! He does not force down the door. That would destroy human freedom. He knocks to be admitted; we alone have the power to unlatch the door to invite Him in, that He may sup with us and we with Him. Christ's greatest sorrow is to be denied admittance. "Ye will not come to me." His greatest joy is to be welcomed even by sinners, for "there is more joy in heaven for one sinner doing penance than for ninety-nine just who need not penance." There is no power as strong as the uplifted hand of an absolving priest; there is no joy like the return of a prodigal; there is no peace like the peace of sin forgiven. There is no hope like the hope the thief gives us: Paradise may still be stolen.

FULTON J. SHEEN

Third Word

"Thy Kingdom come."
"Woman, behold thy son."

When our Lord taught us the "Our Father" He made the third petition a prayer that God's Kingdom, which is the kingdom of saints, might come. Now in His own last prayer He addresses the saintliest of creatures: John the beloved disciple, and Mary His Mother. He was dying on the cross for no other reason than to make us saints—and to be a saint means to be fixed in goodness. The saintliest creature God ever made was the Mother of His divine Son, for she was not only "full of grace" but a co-Redeemer with her Son now suspended above her head. When our Lord looked down to her and commended her to us in the person of John, saying: "Behold thy mother," He was equivalently telling us: "If you wish to be holy, behold thy mother; if you really wish that My Kingdom will come, then behold thy mother; if you will to be rooted in goodness and be perfect as your heavenly Father is perfect, then behold thy mother."

Our Lord made no exception; His Mother was given to all—to those who sin, to those who mourn, and to those who suffer.

Are you a sinner? Then go to Mary, for she knows something of the bitterness of your soul. Mary knows what it is for a soul to be without Jesus, for during the three days loss she merited to become the Refuge of Sinners. She was meriting the honor anew at this very moment. She would never have been given to sinners had there not been a crucifixion, there never would have been a crucifixion without sin, and there never would have been sin without sinners—and where sinners are, there are we. Mary therefore owes the dignity of her title to us, as sinners. Are you a sinner? Then hear her merciful Son lift me from despair with the words: "Behold thy mother."

Are you a mourner? Have you lost a sweet child, a kind father, a loving mother? Then you have lost only part of what you had. But Mary lost everything, for she lost God. To you who mourn: "Behold thy mother."

In moments of unbounded grief, when you are oppressed by your sins, and dripping tears from a wounded or broken heart; when you are sick of what you have and hunger after what you have not; when holiness seems such a distant goal and heaven so far off, then say to Mary: "Remember, Jesus said to thee, concerning me as wicked as I am: 'Woman, behold thy son.'"

Fourth Word

"Thy will be done on earth as it is in heaven."
"My God, my God, why hast thou forsaken me?"

In the "Our Father" Our Lord asked us to resign ourselves to the will of the heavenly Father; on the cross He now resigned Himself to that same divine will. The real lesson hidden in these words is that now and then we face the unintelligible and mysterious things of life and the only solution is to trust in the Will of God. "Thy will be done on earth as it is in heaven." We ask ourselves such questions as: "Why should I suffer? Why did God take away my mother? Why is there pain? Why do the innocent suffer? Why does God abandon me?" There is no answer on earth except: "Thy will be done."

Our Lord in this word is re-emphasizing the lesson taught in the Book of Job. Job was sorely afflicted. He lost his children, his fortune; his wife turned against him, his friends abused him, and his whole body became afflicted with dread. And so he asked the question: "Why?"

"Why did I not die in the womb, why did I not perish when I came out of the belly, why was I received upon the knees, why was I suckled at the breasts; why is light given to him that is in misery, and life to them that are in bitterness of soul?"

Job's friends tried to give him human explanations, to solve all of his riddles, to make everything reasonable, and to show how one part of the universe fits every other part. Now if the Book of Job were a purely human document, a trivial poet or a modern dramatist would have made God enter the scene and answer the questions of Job. And yet when God does come on the scene what does God actually do? He does not answer the questions of Job. He asks Job more questions in a way that abolishes all foolish questions. He turns to Job and says: "Who is this that wrappeth up sentences in unskillful words? Gird up thy loins like a man: I will ask thee, and answer thou me. Where wast thou when I laid the foundations of the earth? ... Upon what are its bases grounded? or who laid the cornerstone thereof... Who shut up the sea with doors, when it broke forth as issuing out of the womb: When I made a cloud the garment thereof, and wrapped it in a mist as in swaddling bands?"

"Then Job answered the Lord, and said I know that thou canst do all things, and no thought is hid from thee... Therefore I have spoken unwisely, and things that above measure exceeded my knowledge."

God insists on the inexplicableness of everything. The Maker of all things is astonished at the things He has made. Instead of proving to Job that it is a world explicable by science, He shows Job that it is a much stranger world than science ever suspected.

The refusal of God to explain His design is itself a burning hint of His design: namely, the riddles of God are more satisfying than the solutions of men. And so, in the Book of Job, we see he was tormented not because he was the worst of men, but because he was the best. It was Good Friday that was prefigured in the wounds of Job.

The lesson for us is that many things are inexplicable here below, but they are only the details, e.g., "Why this pain?" "Why this loss?" "Why this sorrow?" The general principles remain true and unshakable: *God is good, and He wills what is best for the soul.* "My God, why hast thou forsaken me?" means *forsaken* only in appearance, not in reality. We may be lonely, but God is never out of our hearing. Our Lord has gone into the forests of suffering and loneliness, but He has left His footprints there, so we can find the way out. Take God's hand and follow Him in the dark, trusting and believing. We cannot say He does not know what it is to be abandoned for He was abandoned on the cross. "Trust Him when dark doubts assail thee; trust Him when trust is small; trust Him when simply to trust Him is the hardest thing of all."

Fifth Word

"*Give us this day our daily bread.*"
"*I thirst.*"

"Daily bread." At Capharnaum He ministered to the needs of men by giving them food for their bodies. He told men to pray for bread: "Give us this day our daily bread"; but at Calvary He asks for a drink. *Then* He gave His gift to the multitude; *now* the multitude must give their gift. He had been the Giver; now He would be the Receiver. From a torn body He cried, "I thirst." Thirst is the most impatient of all sufferings; there is an imperious urgency about it—a fierce sting.

But it was not just a cry for water. We know that once before He asked the Samaritan woman for a drink, but when she drew the water from the well, there is no record that He took it. He was thirsting for her soul.

The lesson seems to be that *God needs us*. He is *perfect*, and yet He craves our love. He is all-powerful, and yet He is weak without our love. He is infinitely happy and yet unhappy without us. He is the fountain of Everlasting Waters, and yet He cries "I thirst." He does seem to need us. How? Not, of course, in the sense that He is really imperfect, or that He is incomplete without us, but rather *He needs us because we need Him*.

The world is full of such examples. The charitable rich man thirsts for the poor. He does not

need the poor man; from a worldly point of view, the poor man will take part of his substance. The poor man needs him only for food. But the rich man needs the poor man to exercise his charity. Truly can he say: "I thirst." *I need you in order to be kind.* In that sense our Lord thirsts for us, because we need Him so.

He says to us: "I thirst" for you—you the unmortified, because you need my spirit of sacrifice. You who would have a Calvary with hands unscarred and white, have need of my hands that are pierced and red. I am the Redeemer. To you who would never take up a cross, to you who need the spirit of penance, I cry: "I thirst." I thirst for you because your love of pleasure needs my love of sacrifice. I thirst for you, because your love of the world needs my love of heaven. I do not thirst for you because I need you—for without you I never would have had the cross. I do not thirst for you because I need you for my happiness—for without you there would never have been sin. I thirst for you, not because I need you, but because you need me. Why then when I say "I thirst," do you, like the soldier, reach me bitter vinegar and gall?

Sixth Word

"Forgive us our trespasses as we forgive those who trespass against us."
"It is consummated."

Everyone who ever came into the world came into it to live. Our Lord, on the contrary, came not into it to live, but to die. His one supreme task was to lay own His life for the redemption of many.

The forgiving of the trespasses of man by blotting out sin was the unique business His Father had assigned to Him. Now that duty was done. He had made it possible for us to pray "Forgive us our trespasses as we forgive those who trespass against us," and so now He cries out with joy of victory won: "*It is consummated.*"

God labored for six days in the creation of the world, at the end of which came the divine applause of a work completed: "And God saw that it was good." For thirty-three years God, made man, burned with desire to be baptized with the blood of Redemption; and now at the end of the three hours on the cross God saw once more "that it was good." It took only a word to create, but it took a life to redeem.

What a lesson for us! How few of us ever finish the tasks assigned to us. The world is full of souls that are like unfinished symphonies, and half-completed Gothic cathedrals—souls who have begun the poem of their life but have never written the last line; souls that paint pictures and leave out the borders; souls that never have the joy of looking on a perfect work, seeing that it is good, and then, catching an echo from the cross, crying out the song of victory: "It is finished."

Calvary is a place of great impatience. Many souls follow our Lord to the Mount of Beatitudes, but refuse to follow Him to Calvary; some carry their cross to Calvary, but when they get there, they lay it down; some are stripped of the garments of doubt, but refuse to be nailed in the fullness of sacrifice; others are nailed but unfasten themselves before the elevation of the cross; others are crucified but answer the challenge of the world and come down after one hour, after two hours, within a minute of the sound of three. The world is full of half-crucified souls. Few there are who stay until the very end; few there are who know what it is to give all, to see the work well done, and experience the thrill of a victory won. Would that there were a single day in our life, in which we could honestly say—I have given God all! "It is finished."

Seventh Word

"Deliver us from all evil. Amen."
"Father, into thy hands I commend my spirit."

There is no deliverance from evil except in heaven. That too is why the final petition of the "Our Father" which asks that we be delivered from evil is balanced by the last words of our Lord from the cross commending His Soul into the hands of His Heavenly Father.

There is evil in the world, and as long as we remain here below we must struggle against it. God might have made a different world, a world in which we would have sprouted virtue by the same necessity that the sun rises, and fire burns, and iron is hard. But then where would merit and character have been? All life is a trial. I can be one of God's heroes only because I might have been one of God's cowards; I can be one of the patriots of the Kingdom of God, only because I might have been one of its traitors; I can be a saint of the cross only because I might also be a devil. There is no epic of the certainties of life; no crowns of merit rest suspended over those who do not fight; there are no aureoles except for those who might have turned back and yet pushed on.

Christ's eyes now look downward as the last few drops of blood reluctantly wed themselves to the rocks, splitting them open like hungry mouths. There is always a strange power in the eyes of the dying, which enables them to follow the ones they love, even when other senses are mute and dead. His eyes are now resting on the same object He rested on when He was born—His sweet and beloved Mother. She felt His eyes fixed on her. She looked up, the eyes closed, the head dropped, there was the rupture of a heart through the rapture of love, and there Mary stood beneath the cross—a childless Mother, bereaved of God.

Sleep on tired world! Your God is dead. Sleep on creatures! You now have creation to yourself. Sleep on Jerusalem! You have slain the Prophet who would have made you a Heavenly City. Sleep on sinners! The Heart that filled you with remorse is pierced with a lance. Sleep on, all ye who hate, for the wings of love are broken. Sleep on atheists, you have killed your God. Sleep in your false sleep—you can do more than nature can, for it awakes and shudders at your crime. Sleep on for your few brief moments but remember some day you will awaken and one vision will meet your eyes: The Vision of Love Crucified on a cross.

May you throw yourself beneath it and in the ecstasy of knowing God as your Father may you pray the prayer of Salvation: "Our Father, who art in heaven—like thy Son—into thy hands I commend my spirit."

* * *

THE HEAVENLY EASTER

DELIVERED ON APRIL 21, 1935

TODAY we conclude our series on the "Fullness of Christ." For my subject I am going to speak about two words found in St. Paul: one, "emptying"; the other word, "filling." St. Paul speaks of Christ emptying Himself, and also of the Church as being the "fullness of Christ." These words can both be applied to the historical life of our Lord, in the sense that Good Friday was the "emptying" of His divine majesty and Easter Sunday its "filling up" in the glory of the Resurrection. But I am going to correlate the cross and the crown not in relation to those three days, but to the great cosmic plan, which embraces time and eternity, the Good Friday of creation and the Easter Sunday of Heaven.

First of all, the history of God emptying Himself. All goodness empties itself in the sense that it tends to diffuse and to communicate its goodness. The sun is good, and it empties itself in light and heat; the flowers are good, and they empty themselves in the riotous colors of their petals and the perfume of their silken chalices; animals are good, and they empty themselves in the generation of their young; man is good and he empties himself in the communication of thoughts, and above all else by sacrifice, born and begotten of unselfish love. Now God is Perfect Goodness, for He possesses within Himself the fullness of Life, of Truth, and of Love in the amiable society of the Father, Son, and Holy Ghost. Being goodness itself we should therefore expect Him to diffuse and communicate His Goodness.

That process by which divine love opened the Fountains of the Godhead and poured them out is called by St. Paul the emptying of God—not an emptying in the sense that He lost what He gave, for He no more lost His Perfection by giving than we lose anything by loving our friends, or by looking at our image in a mirror. Rather, He emptied Himself in the sense that others began to share that which before was unshared.

Divine Love did not empty itself all at once. Only progressively through the ages did Love pour itself out in ever increasing draughts until He had given all. He permitted creatures furtive glances behind the curtain of His divinity, for the complete vision if given all at once would have been too great for man, as a bright light sometimes blinds rather than illumines. The first outpouring of the chalice of divine love was at the beginning of time. Love could not contain the torrents of its Power and Goodness, and He emptied Himself of them and told them to nothingness: That was Creation. Love could not keep the secrets of His Heart so He emptied Himself of them and told them to men: That was Revelation. Love tends to become like the one loved; God loved man, and so He emptied Himself and was found in the form and habit of man: That was the Incarnation. Love also gives itself to the one loved, and if need be suffers and dies, for greater love than this no man hath that he lay down his life for his friends: That was Redemption.

Love by its very nature tends to unity, not only in the flesh but in the spirit. Unity in the flesh was the Incarnation. The final emptying of divine love came when He poured out not His Blood on the cross, but His Spirit on the Church on the day of Pentecost. That was the birth of His Mystical Body.

There was nothing more that divine love could do. He had emptied Himself of His power and wisdom in Creation, of His secrets in Revelation, of His majesty in the Incarnation, of His Body and Blood in the Redemption, and of His Spirit in the Church. Well indeed might Love say: "What more can I do for my vineyard than I have done? From the Chalice of my Love I have poured forth even the last drop. I have kept back nothing. I have given you all that is mine as God." Truly indeed might St. Paul say: *He emptied Himself.*

But now let us look at the other side of the picture. All love is reciprocal. I love and I am loved. The love which spends itself is to be loved in return, for every emptying implies a filling. The emptying of the river calls for the filling of the ocean: The emptying of the valleys demands the fullness of the mountains: the emptying of the strength, youth, and life blood of parents is filled by the charms and radiance of their children. Everywhere the story is the same. The cross cries out to the grave, the humiliation to the exaltation, and the Good Friday to the Easter Sunday. The reason is obvious: Love is not sterile, but a patient usurer who gets back his own in time. If then love is fecund and productive; if love by its very nature cries out for love in return, then surely the divine love that empties itself must be filled. The downward course of His Love striking the mirror of our hearts must be reflected back again in heaven. Then, like the planets which travel in orbits, the divine love that was sent out to the circle of this universe would once more return to its starting point filled with the myriad loves of creatures it met on the way. If God has emptied Himself of divine love then He should be filled with it in the hearts of men; if He has poured forth then He should be replenished; if He has drained His Chalice, then it should be filled again. And at this point begins the history of the filling; or the story of how man loved God because God first loved men. If the story of the "emptying" of God stretches in history from the Creation to the descent of the holy Ghost, then the story of the filling reaches from the descent of the Holy Ghost to the final glorification of the Kingdom of Heaven, or the return of Prodigal Love back again to the Father's House. In a word, the growth of the Mystical Body of Christ is the story of the "filling up" of Christ to His full stature in the glory of the celestial Jerusalem.

And these are the stages of the "filling." The love of God that emptied itself in Creation is filled as the Church lays hold of material things, breathes over them the words "Praise ye the Lord," and thus makes them pay tribute to the Creator. The gold in the bowels of the earth, the wheat in the field, the grapes in the vineyard, the trees of the forest, cannot of themselves thank God, but the Church by putting gold in the Chalice, wheat and grapes in her Mass, wood in the crucifixes, thus "fills up" unto God the very Love that He once poured out in their creation.

The love of God that emptied Itself of His secrets in Revelation, is filled up by the faith of the Church in the three hundred million Catholics throughout the world who chant her Credo and profess unto death that they believe every truth Christ teaches "because He can neither deceive nor be deceived."

The Love that emptied itself in the Incarnation by God becoming man, is now filled and returned by the Church, by whose sacraments men become adopted sons of the Father partaking of the nature of our Lord and Savior Jesus Christ.

The Love that emptied itself in the outpouring of the Spirit of God on the day of Pentecost is now filled up by the Church, by the incorporating to that Spirit of millions and millions of souls who for twenty centuries have lived the life of the One Body, have been vivified by the same Spirit, and have been obedient to the one Head.

If you would know the extent of the growth of the fullness of Christ in His Mystical Body, then think of how much a human organism grows from the moment of conception. In the course of its life millions and millions of cells have been unified and vivified by the soul which came into the original cell at the moment of its origin. But even that is an inadequate picture of the growth of the Mystical Body of Christ, for the soul of man leaves the body, but the Holy Ghost never leaves the Church. There is no adequate human analogy for what St. Paul calls the fullness of Christ, which is the Church. There is no way of adequately measuring the amount of faith, of hope, and of love that has been returned by the Church to God since the day of Pentecost. But since the Church is a living personality, because it has the same Soul, the same Head, the same Mind, the same Heart, the same Life now as it had nineteen hundred years ago, she can tell us of her growth and fullness in the first person.

And these are the words of the Church on the fullness of Christ: "On the day of Pentecost there were twelve cells in my Body besides the Blessed Mother who was left to be my mother and nurse during infancy. My Body first began to grow within the nursery of Judaism where I had my birth; but within a few short years I had incorporated unto myself even the Gentiles who knew no God but Caesar. My Spouse, Christ, had told me that I would be hated as He was hated, and while still an infant there were other Herods who would have slain me in Rome, as they would have slain Him in Bethlehem. I have had but few moments of peace. From the outside I was attacked by the sword; from the inside I was abused by false brethren. And yet neither persecution nor error has stopped my growth. The sword strengthened my courage, and error sharpened my intellect. In a century I had grown until I filled the Roman empire, and then beyond its outposts I sent forth missionaries to the barbarians who helped me grow unto that fullness I had when I crowned Charlemagne in the year 800. My Body grew in age and grace and strength and in the twelfth century of my existence, like Christ in His twelfth year, I was instructing the Doctors of the world in the temples of the medieval universities. In the sixteenth century I lost some cells of my Body, as I had lost some before in the errors of the Gnostics and Pelagians. And yet after each loss there came new strength, for my lot, like that of my Spouse Christ, is to be ever rising from the tomb where men leave me as dead. And so I chastened myself at the Council of Trent and brought myself into subjection, and now at this very hour the twelve cells whom I numbered in my Body on Pentecost have grown to three hundred million souls in every corner of the globe.

"But in the course of my life of nineteen hundred years, like the life of a human body, some of my cells have died and been replaced by others—but I have remained the same, because my soul is the abiding Spirit of God. Some of my members have been gathered into the Church Triumphant, where they enjoy blessedness with my Spouse Christ; others of my members who, while they were with me in the Church Militant, sinned and atoned not, are now gathered in Purgatory which is the Church Suffering where they wash their baptismal robes clear for the Spotless King in the glory of Heaven. How much longer I shall live on this earth, how much time awaits the consummation, I know not. But when the number of the elect is completed, when the seats vacated by the fallen angels are filled, when I shall have grown to my full stature, then shall the end come; then shall the Church militant on earth and the Church suffering in Purgatory be gathered into the unity of the Church triumphant in Heaven, on the glorious Easter that shall never end because there is no time with God but only eternal Love. And would you know the fullness of Christ; would you know the final end of the Mystical Body of Christ; would you know what will happen on that Easter Day when Christ the Head and I His Body are united in heaven? Then listen to my words as I set them down through John in the Apocalypse: I saw a new heaven and a new earth. And I saw the holy city, the new Jerusalem coming down out of heaven from God prepared as a bride adorned for her husband. And I heard a great voice from the throne saying: Behold the tabernacle of God with men, and he will dwell with them. And they shall be his people; and God himself with them shall be their God. And God shall wipe away all tears from their eyes; and death shall be no more, nor mourning, nor crying, nor sorrow shall be any more, for the former things are passed away... And he showed me the holy city of Jerusalem coming down out of heaven from God, having the glory of God, and the light thereof was like to a precious stone as to the jasper stone, even as crystal. And it had a wall great and high, having twelve gates, and in the gates twelve angels, and names written thereon, which are the names of the twelve tribes of the children of Israel. On the east, three gates; and on the north, three gates; and on the south, three gates; and on the west, three gates. And the wall of the city had twelve foundations, and in them, the twelve names of the twelve apostles of the Lamb... And the building of the wall thereof was of jasper stone: but the city itself pure gold, like to clear glass. And the foundations of the walls of the city were adorned with all manner of precious stones... And the twelve gates are twelve pearls, one to each... and the street of the city was pure gold, as it were transparent glass. And I saw no temple therein. For the Lord Almighty is the temple thereof and the Lamb. And the city hath no need of the sun, nor of the moon, to shine in it. For the glory of God hath enlightened it, and the Lamb is the lamp thereof."

"And I saw a great multitude which no man could number of all nations, and tribes, and peoples, and tongues, standing before the throne, and in sight of the Lamb, clothed with white robes and palms in their hands: And they cried with a loud voice saying: Salvation to our God, who sitteth upon the throne, and to the Lamb. And all the angels stood round about the throne, and the ancients, and the four living creatures: and they fell down upon their faces, and adored God, saying: Amen. Benediction and glory, and wisdom, and thanksgiving, honor and power and strength to our God for ever and ever. Amen"

Such is the end and destiny of the Church which St. Paul describes as the fullness of Christ. It was born of the emptying of God's love; it is filled by all the virgins and martyrs, confessors and pontiffs, saintly mothers and fathers, devoted husbands and wives, sacrificing missionaries and apostolic priests, simple children who never grew wise with the false wisdom of the world, and all members of Christ's Mystical Body who filled up once again with Love the divine chalice, which Love drained in making and redeeming us. Thus the end of the Chapter of Time will be when the Mystical Body of Christ, which is His Church, will have grown to its fullness, just as the glory of the physical body of Christ came when it had reached its fullness in its Good Friday and Easter Sunday; the end of history will come at the moment when Love which came down from heaven in an Emmanuel disguised in lowliness, becomes transfigured in its fullness as the Church, the glory of the Great Original, the Lamb of God who taketh away the sins of the world: Evil will end when the last baptized child, hewn from the great quarry

THE CHRIST

of humanity, shall be shaped and squared and cut for service in the great living Temple whose architect is Love—which is God.

Cardinal Hayes States Purpose of Catholic Hour
EXTRACT FROM HIS ADDRESS AT THE INAUGURAL PROGRAM
IN THE STUDIO OF THE NATIONAL BROADCASTING COMPANY
NEW YORK CITY, MARCH 2, 1930

Our congratulations and our gratitude are extended to the National Council of Catholic Men and its officials, and to all who, by their financial support, have made it possible to use this offer of the National Broadcasting Company. The heavy expense of managing and financing a weekly program, its musical numbers, its speakers, the subsequent answering of inquiries, must be met.

This radio hour is for all the people of the United States. To our fellow-citizens, in this word of dedication, we wish to express a cordial greeting and, indeed, congratulations. For this radio hour is one of service to America, which certainly will listen in interestedly, and even sympathetically, I am sure, to the voice of the ancient Church with its historic background of all the centuries of the Christian era, and with its own notable contribution to the discovery, exploration, foundation and growth of our glorious country.

Thus to voice before a vast public the Catholic Church is no light task. Our prayers will be with those who have that task in hand. We feel certain that it will have both the good will and the good wishes of the great majority of our countrymen. Surely, there is no true lover of our Country who does not eagerly hope for a less worldly, a less material, and a more spiritual standard among our people.

With good will, with kindness and with Christ-like sympathy for all, this work is inaugurated. So may it continue. So may it be fulfilled. This word of dedication voices, therefore, the hope that this radio hour may serve to make known, to explain with the charity of Christ, our faith, which we love even as we love Christ Himself. May it serve to make better understood that faith as it really is—a light revealing the pathway to heaven: a strength, and a power divine through Christ; pardoning our sins, elevating, consecrating our common every-day duties and joys, bringing not only justice but gladness and peace to our searching and questioning hearts.

Made in the USA
Monee, IL
25 January 2025

10048961R00154